T0294527

Museum Accessibility by Design

AMERICAN ALLIANCE OF MUSEUMS

The American Alliance of Museums has been bringing museums together since 1906, helping to develop standards and best practices, gathering and sharing knowledge, and providing advocacy on issues of concern to the entire museum community. Representing more than 35,000 individual museum professionals and volunteers, institutions, and corporate partners serving the museum field, the Alliance stands for the broad scope of the museum community.

The American Alliance of Museums' mission is to champion museums and nurture excellence in partnership with its members and allies.

Books published by AAM further the Alliance's mission to make standards and best practices for the broad museum community widely available.

American Alliance of Museums

Museum Accessibility by Design

A Systemic Approach to Organizational Change

Maria Chiara Ciaccheri

ROWMAN & LITTLEFIELD
Lanham • Boulder • New York • London

Published by Rowman & Littlefield
An imprint of The Rowman & Littlefield Publishing Group, Inc.
4501 Forbes Boulevard, Suite 200, Lanham, Maryland 20706
www.rowman.com

86-90 Paul Street, London EC2A 4NE

Copyright © 2022 by American Alliance of Museums

All rights reserved. No part of this book may be reproduced in any form or by any electronic or mechanical means, including information storage and retrieval systems, without written permission from the publisher, except by a reviewer who may quote passages in a review.

British Library Cataloguing in Publication Information Available

Library of Congress Cataloging-in-Publication Data

Names: Ciaccheri, Maria Chiara, 1981- author.
Title: Museum accessibility by design : a systemic approach to
  organizational change / Maria Chiara Ciaccheri.
Description: Lanham : Rowman & Littlefield, 2022. | Includes
  bibliographical references and index.
Identifiers: LCCN 2022001198 (print) | LCCN 2022001199 (ebook) | ISBN
  9781538156025 (cloth) | ISBN 9781538156032 (paperback) | ISBN
  9781538156049 (ebook)
Subjects: LCSH: Museums and people with disabilities.
Classification: LCC AM160 .C53 2022 (print) | LCC AM160 (ebook) | DDC
  069/.17—dc23/eng/20220118
LC record available at https://lccn.loc.gov/2022001198
LC ebook record available at https://lccn.loc.gov/2022001199

♾️™ The paper used in this publication meets the minimum requirements of American National Standard for Information Sciences—Permanence of Paper for Printed Library Materials, ANSI/NISO Z39.48-1992.

To Anna and Zeno.

Contents

Contents

Foreword

Access to arts, culture, history, and science is a human right, and museums have a public and social responsibility to provide access to all—free of discrimination, exclusion, and barriers. Yet so few institutions place this deeply human responsibility at the center of their practice. With the recent demand for more diversity, equity, and inclusion across the museum field, we have seen some positive changes happening—yet issues of access and accessibility are so frequently separated out and treated like something categorically different than foundational equity work. Many museums have added "accessibility" to their language and acronyms (DEIA or IDEA) around equity; however, efforts to address the widespread barriers that create inaccessibility remain limited to a series of legally required accommodations, programs, or services. There continues to be a highly problematic gap between museums proclaiming "access" as a core principle, and the actual experience of "access" for so many people visiting museums each and every day.

The pages that follow provide a much-needed discussion of the complex discipline of museum accessibility. Through these chapters, Ciaccheri presents a clear picture of the resistance and barriers holding this work back, and she offers practical strategies to shift our mindset and advocate for a deeper and more holistic approach to accessibility in museums. Museums need to move past a narrow focus on physical and architectural barriers, Ciaccheri argues, and instead embrace a deeper culture of accessibility across the entire institution—one that "sees the museum as an interconnected organism capable of responding to different human needs."

As someone who has advocated for accessibility within museums throughout my entire career, I understand many of the immense challenges involved in this work. And as someone who does not identify as living with disability, I also understand that I have been a part of maintaining barriers and causing harm through my role within institutions where ableism is pervasive. There is no easy fix to the barriers—physical and cognitive, as well as cultural, economic, linguistic, and technological—facing so many of our museum visitors, staff, and volunteers. As this book argues, access is a deep and ongoing process that transforms a museum's culture in every aspect and in every area of its operations. This work involves constant listening and learning, disrupting stereotypes and false assumptions, developing trust, and building relationships. We need to continuously invest in these forms of human-centered work if we are to permanently dismantle the conditions that create inaccessibility.

In her opening keynote at the 2018 Disability Intersectionality Summit, activist and writer Alice Wong shared these powerful words:

> Access for the sake of access or inclusion is not necessarily liberatory, but access done in the service of love, justice, connection, and community is liberatory and has the power to transform.

The challenges of our time have given us the perfect opportunity to radically rethink museums and create a path forward that is grounded in this type of liberatory access. Through its research, resources, case studies, and strategies, this book provides you with a roadmap to begin this journey. It is up to each of us—as museum workers, leaders, visitors, community members, and engaged citizens—to make the choice to demand better and be a part of making this transformation happen, starting right now. A more accessible future is possible, and it is up to us to make this happen together.

—Mike Murawski

Acknowledgments

The opportunity to write this book was huge, and I thank American Alliance of Museums for the trust.

Everything contained in this volume is the result of years of exchanges, discussions, and conversations with Italian and foreign colleagues: to all of them goes my most sincere gratitude. I would like to thank Cristina Seveso, with whom I worked for many years around issues of equality, diversity, and inclusion. That milieu, made up mainly of volunteers, helped me understand the importance of maintaining a positive predisposition and cultivating meaningful relationships. This is how I discovered my vocation for museum accessibility. Thanks also go to my colleagues at ABCittà who have given me space for writing at the expense of shared projects, and moreover for the opportunity to learn what participation means over the course of our ten-year collaboration. Among them, Anna Chiara Cimoli has become one of my mentors through her passion and knowledge of museums and social justice issues. Thanks also to Nicolas D'Oronzio, Nicole Moolhuijsen, and WeExhibit for the space they have granted me to approach accessibility from stimulating and rigorous perspectives. Thanks, too, to the colleagues from different organizations and museums who more recently have trusted and accompanied me in rising to contemporary challenges of the field with a focus on strategies and policies development.

The generosity and expertise of colleagues and friends like Alessandra Gariboldi, Maria Elena Colombo, and Paola Boccalatte has also been very important, together with what I learned from many others, such as Valeria Bottalico, Silvia Mascheroni, Simona Bodo, Guido Vaglio, Cristina Alga, Miriam Mandosi, Lorenza Salati, Giulia Grechi, Francesco Mannino, Annamaria Cilento, Paola Rampoldi, Davide Ianni, Marta Vireca, Eleonora Moro, Antonio Panella, and Annalisa Trasatti, just to mention a few.

I would like to thank the colleagues who made themselves available, especially to verify references mentioned in this book: Lara Schweller, Nelly Ekstrom, Ellysheva Zeira, Rebecca Granados, Paul Molinari, Jill Bernstein, Bojana Coklyat, Clint Curle, Christian Adame, and Christine Reich. Many thanks to Rebecca McGinnis, Marie Clapot, Catterina Seia, Danielle Linzer, Sina Barham, Christena M. Gunther, Cristina Bucci, Lucia Cominoli, Irene Balzani, and Betty Siegel also, because their work, for different reasons, has offered so much inspiration to me.

Thanks to Charles Harmon, my editor at Rowman & Littlefield, without whom I would still be rewriting the first chapter and who spurred me on to do my best. Thanks also to Dominique McIndoe, production editor, for her valuable assistance.

Huge thanks to Mike Murawski for his kindness in writing such a supportive foreword and whose valuable work is cultivating transformation in museums world-wide, helping colleagues envision and enact change and inclusion.

Much of my interest and awareness around accessibility stems from my family, made up of people extremely diverse in needs, interests, and experiences. To my parents, infinite thanks for passing on to me an enthusiasm for museums, but above all for supporting all my choices, especially those that involved travel. Thanks to my aunts, who, in the last two years of the pandemic, encouraged this work from afar. Thanks especially to Remo. Our son Zeno's arrival coincided with this book's development: a journey that confirms every day his generosity and sense of humor, as well as the strength of our bond.

Finally, many thanks to Catriona McLead, for her proofreading expertise, and to Yvonne A. Mazurek, whose editorial support was crucial.

Obviously, the many people who have given me their time and support over the years cannot be contained in these short paragraphs. This list would also need to include all the authors whose texts have changed my perspective on accessibility and museums. Thanks to this vibrant community, I imagine that my thoughts will continue to evolve over time, spurred by questions and future encounters with other people's perspectives and experiences.

Preface

What does it mean to talk about museum accessibility today? How can accessibility promote change in cultural organizations and in society at large? What kind of change can we hope to achieve? And what concrete actions can we undertake to make this change happen? *Museum Accessibility by Design: A Systemic Approach to Organizational Change* explores the complex subject of museum accessibility, a discipline whose purpose is to break down barriers by facilitating access and possibly autonomy for as many people as possible in museums.

For a number of years, many cultural institutions have viewed access as an issue of critical importance, yet the discussions remain problematic. The topic is increasingly present at conferences, and specialized courses are expanding, while more and more institutions are investing resources in this area. Nonetheless, the discipline still struggles to establish itself and suffers from the fallout of prejudices that are sometimes rooted in these very organizations. To this day, *museum accessibility* is a term mainly used in reference to an assortment of services and facilities that ensure access for people with disabilities. Even when institutions adopt good practices—often in full compliance with local legal requirements—the discipline continues to be hampered by internal resistance that prevents it from becoming an essential subject matter, even though it is one of the most effective means through which museums establish meaningful relationships with visitors. This phenomenon, evident in museums worldwide, also stems from a stereotypical perception that unfortunately restricts its dissemination. One of the most widespread stereotypes, for example, is the idea that accessibility only benefits a small minority: a concept that also indirectly leads to the thought that people with disabilities lack autonomy and demonstrate more needs than others. This idea characterizes just one of the many clichés that facilitate a distorted understanding of accessibility and give rise to approaches that go beyond museum contexts.

Although these ambiguities are evident, we are seeing recent and profound changes unfolding in the field of accessibility, giving rise to new questions and awareness around different models, their application, and their potential impact on museums and many other contexts. While the term *accessibility* was formerly used almost exclusively to refer to a series of circumscribed tools or services (from a tactile reproduction of an artwork to ways of involving caregivers in a workshop for visitors with Alzheimer's), we now know that museums must first acquire a macroscopic understanding of the discipline in order to foster real, people-oriented change. In fact, museum accessibility is needed on many levels, and, above all, it requires action at the organizational level. Rather than being made up of small, incremental educational or architectural achievements, accessibility deserves to be seen as an ongoing and long-term process to be integrated across the board to offer extensive and visible benefits to every visitor's experience. For this reason, we must rethink our methods and adopt fresh theories and training solutions that allow a new culture of accessibility to assert itself. The effort required is less than one might expect, and its outcomes offer great rewards.

Museums have traditionally been seen as places for learning about "high culture": spaces reserved for a select few. Today we must insist that these institutions become spaces characterized by democracy and openness. This transformation is still inevitably marked by persistent contradictions: Museum contexts require anyone to walk, observe, and engage with spaces and strategies that are often far from an accessible mindset. On the one hand, most museums remain inaccessible; on the other hand, accessibility is usually constrained by limited space and time. In all cases, usability is rarely considered as a shared need, equality is only partly realized, and access risks are relegated to a philanthropic dimension rather than museums grasping their true value and utility.

This book results from fifteen years of experience in the field of museum design and teaching: a relatively short time in the grand scheme of things, but long enough to have witnessed hundreds of cases, strategies, and best practices firsthand, both in my daily work in Italy, my home country, and in the United States, where I lived on and off for two years, engaging in research and professional development in this area. On a personal level, my family's experience with these issues deeply informed my understanding of disability and access. In addition to my extensive experience working with people with intellectual disabilities and in the field of participatory design, another key component of my background is a master's degree in learning and visitor studies in museums from the School of Museum Studies at the University of Leicester in the UK, an institution with an established commitment to disability representation research. Perhaps the most significant experience was a visiting fellowship in 2014 that took me to several major US cities where I visited over a hundred museums and interviewed an equal number of colleagues from institutions with groundbreaking approaches to accessibility. While the resulting pieces I published are due for an update, that research constitutes a solid foundation for understanding the phenomena that are evident across the country to this day.

There is no doubt that Italy and the United States differ in terms of experience, regulations, and the diffusion of accessibility, but the divergences observed across these geographical contexts have proved enormously valuable. With this in mind, I included case studies from other countries to impart a broader vision and greater complexity to this book; all the while, the geographical scope has deliberately focused on case studies from museums from the so-called West. I made this decision conscientiously to fall back on my own experience of and familiarity with certain sociocultural perspectives, perceptions of disability, and meanings attributed to accessibility.

According to Umberto Eco, a cultured person is not one who has read all the books in the world, but one who knows how to move between bookshelves, someone capable of mastering knowledge without needing to possess it all. Similarly, this volume aims to help readers (students, professionals, or simply those interested) orient themselves in a structured and, at times, seemingly contradictory terrain, suggesting the adoption of a systemic approach that sees the museum as an interconnected organism capable of responding to different human needs. This is why this book encourages greater cooperation between those concerned with visitors' experience and those working on accessibility as a means to improve museum access for all, but especially for people with disabilities. In these terms, accessibility has the potential to break free of its conventional confines, with a focus toward the process and, above all, the vision of the museum as an inclusive whole.

In particular, this text aims to offer a critical and probing perspective on museum accessibility, an approach gleaned from personal observations, targeted research, and direct exchanges with recipients: visitors, non-visitors, activists, and colleagues, with and without disabilities. By reframing accessibility as an enduring process that is rooted in the institutional, museums can reach the broadest possible spectrum of people and cultivate opportunities for dialogue and co-design. This process is, of course, never easy; it requires a step-by-step approach that is considerate of museums' often-limited resources and realistic about ways in which museum staff, leaders, and decision-makers may face such changes with a lack of interest or resistance.

Therefore, *Museum Accessibility by Design* explores accessibility in stages and prompts discussion through questions. It integrates a more traditional view of the subject with often-neglected points that prove crucial for understanding why accessibility is a fundamental discipline, and why its development has been impeded. Divided into two parts, the first half of the book begins with a theoretical introduction, which then branches into suggestions for staff training with plenty of practical guidance and structured activities.

Here are the book's key characteristics:

1. The text broadens the concept of access and offers suggestions for its development within museums. It considers a variety of constraints while delving into critical learning and strategies designed to break down common prejudices. It looks at accessibility from a user-design perspective, in which the museum experience revolves around visitors and any needs, desires, and motivations they may have, whether their needs are permanent, temporary, or situational. Accessibility is valuable not only because it facilitates everyone's experience

but also because it nudges people's behavior in predictable and constructive ways. For this reason, the volume also places significant emphasis on usability, attention renewal, and other key cognitive issues that are usually excluded from the conversation around accessibility: topics that, in this field, are equally essential, despite being more prevalent in design studies and environmental psychology.

2. Accessibility is not for the sole benefit of people with disabilities. While fully espousing the social model whereby context contributes substantially to the definition of disability, the book takes a more analytical, interdisciplinary, and multifaceted look both at people and at barriers. Disability finds many obstacles in today's world: The disadvantages encountered by this group are certainly evident and need to be dismantled through specific actions. At the same time, however, any classification represents a theoretical and cultural assumption that tends to look at people through a limited lens and risks oversimplifying valuable complexities: for example, in terms of age, interests, motivation. Disability is a way of being in the world, and accessibility, in the conventional sense of the word, cannot promote inclusion alone. On this basis, this book asks whether it is necessary to adopt a new, more spontaneous approach to disability while addressing accessibility more rigorously. For this reason, the book mentions disability frequently, but it refers to audiences in the broadest sense of the term.

3. This volume promotes a systemic perspective that allows readers to see museum accessibility as a cultural process addressed to answer multiple and overlapped needs rather than an incremental adoption of singular guidelines for a few. Even a small action implemented by a museum needs to be part of a strategic framework that establishes shared policies. This process needs to ground itself in context analysis, clearly defined goals, and plans for their implementation. Accessibility cannot be left solely to educators or experts in the field: Entire institutions, with the help of accessibility project managers, should harbor the common objectives that demarcate boundaries and expand mutual responsibilities.

4. This book proposes an operational and not merely theoretical approach to museum accessibility. It suggests concrete activities like structured workshops with step-by-step staff training and provides specific examples and good practices from different parts of the world.

In short, this volume sets out to affirm accessibility as a shared, indispensable, and systemwide endeavor. This belief urges cultural institutions to see themselves from the outside in: Are museums perceived as exclusionary institutions? If so, to what extent?

Well before the adoption of best practices, there is the need to generate a proactive attitude that insists on people's similarities. It is only through the espousal of new prospects that we can recognize the fundamental importance of accessibility.

Doing so can help dismantle stigmas about disability that sometimes can paradoxically be fueled in the name of access. Museums have the power to promote a new awareness and set an example for society as a whole.

Making museums more accessible is about encouraging exchange between different people and, in the case of disability, boosting visibility. In many countries, disability is still considered a source of shame, and it solicits pitying glances and compassion. Part of a museum's responsibility is to normalize this condition as much as possible and make room for it to exist among the many elements that define diversity. Making these institutions more accessible entails empowering the entire staff through careful planning, starting with research and discussion.

Such change is already underway, and it is up to us to keep the flame kindled. We just might be the right person, in the right place, at the right time. When we each grasp our social responsibility, whatever and wherever that may be, we are actively partaking in a better future that accessibility can help to forge.

Part I

Museum Accessibility as a Systemic Discipline

The growing interest in museum accessibility implies that an increasing number of people recognize and view the subject as a discipline. This work poses one of the most significant challenges for museums around the world, and we can observe a particular urgency in countries where audiences play a central role in the dominant professional discourse.

The first half of this book takes a theoretical look at the discipline, guiding the reader through its complexities to instill a broader and more critical understanding of the subject. The purpose of this section is to highlight the need for accessibility to be fully adopted by cultural institutions while calling into question certain aspects that are often taken for granted, limiting progress in this area. The topic will be analyzed following an inclusive approach, with strategies aimed at reaching as many people as possible. Transversal participation is a theme that will emerge throughout this discussion. The text also emphasizes the importance of an interdisciplinary perspective that sees accessibility through the holistic analysis of a visitor's experience that pays particular attention to their cognition of a visit. To make these considerations more evident, readers are taken through a series of reflections that intend to question linear interpretations in favor of an equally coherent and more complex comprehension.

The first chapter outlines the subjects' origins as a grassroots movement responding to the needs of people with disabilities dating back to the 1970s. This part introduces the topic through a more traditional analysis and highlights key aspects like the role of disability studies and the impact of legislation, which prove essential for understanding the development of the discipline in different countries.

While the first chapter clarifies basics, the second defines a broader framework. The focus here is on the cognitive effects of a museum experience, so as to encourage museums to foster engagement through multimodal approaches and a variety of interpretive strategies that lever people's attention and motivation. The scope of the second chapter is, therefore, to encourage museums to cultivate a deeper culture of accessibility based on awareness rather than on mere adherence to a rigid set of rules. This reflection reveals the way in which accessibility can be manifested—or not—through a series of complex interactions between visitors and museums.

The third chapter switches from the museum's perspective to that of the visitors themselves, seeking to dispel common myths and misconceptions. This visitor-focused perspective enables us to recognize a museum's responsibility to address specific needs. Furthermore, it places the needs of people with and without disabilities at the center of the analysis.

The fourth chapter presents variations of themes presented earlier by delving into the digital realm and reminds us, in the midst of a pandemic, that a museum's material boundaries are essentially relative. This discussion concentrates less on process and more on solutions by way of example to focus on a less-evident skill set, like understanding visitors' individual complexities and finding apt solutions to second their autonomous exploration.

The fifth chapter summarizes some of the ideas discussed above, while examining forms of resistance and major limitations that hinder the growth and diffusion of accessibility. This section begins with a brief articulation of the topic, as well as the factors that curb its development in the museum world. This section goes on to explore recurring prejudices that unfortunately define the field. These forms of discrimination are often overlooked in the international debate but are of vital importance in devising effective strategies for future development.

The conclusion of the first half of the book introduces new approaches to accessibility and rethinks the discipline from a strategic and processual perspective. This sixth chapter deals more specifically with methodologies and functional choices that can be deployed by drawing from inclusive design and theories of systemic thinking. This reflection marks a transition to the second part of the book, which details operational phases and staff training exercises that aim to establish strategic and process-led approaches at all levels of museum work.

1

Museum Accessibility

A HISTORICAL AND SOCIAL ACHIEVEMENT

Accessibility marks the intersection between the history of museums and the commitment to provide equal access opportunities to as many people as possible. Over time, it has become an area of research and practice capable of improving the visitor experience. While its development in Western countries is relatively recent, this interdisciplinary subject is well underway, albeit in a fragmentary manner. As with any dynamic discipline, its significance remains open to a variety of inter-pretations. In other words, it "means different things to different people."[1] In fact, defining *accessibility* continues to oscillate between the most prevalent reference to people with disabilities and a broader proposition addressed "to everyone along the continuum of human ability and experience," as stated by the American Alliance of Museums.[2] Helen Graham calls it "a general way to manage the mediation between museums' collections and all potential visitors,"[3] while the designer Kat Holmes conceives *accessibility* as "the qualities that make an experience open to all."[4] In this volume, the discipline will be considered primarily as a process that requires not only tools and skills, but more importantly, a long-term-oriented strategy that starts from the ground up. Its catalyst lies in the recognition of different human needs, and its ultimate aim is to take down the many barriers to promote nondiscriminatory participation.

It is no coincidence that its introduction into museums took place just as these cultural institutions began to transform on several fronts. Since the seventies, in fact, there has been a shift "from being about something to being for somebody";[5] this shift marks a more flexible approach in terms of facilitation and open access, as well as the need to affirm the importance to such concepts as representation, authority, and power—recurrent themes in this investigation.[6]

This progressive change has not been linear and it continues to develop. Museums are slowly opening themselves up to different audiences, which is due both to a growing general awareness, as well as to debates taking place within the field. They listen while remaining porous and sensitive.[7] Increasingly, they are spokespeople for sensibilities or even social injustices present outside their walls.

In this light, it is essential to contextualize accessibility within history alongside a social and cultural understanding of disability. In fact, even when accessibility is conceived in a broader way, aimed at the inclusion of as many people as possible, it is important to remember that this field emerged directly from people with disabilities advocating for their own rights. This discipline has transformed the perception of disability itself. By reflecting on its foundations, it becomes easier to articulate key aspects through disability studies and to highlight ways in which normative contributions have promoted the development of accessibility in some countries more than others.

FROM SOCIETY TO MUSEUMS

Although the perception of disability has evolved over time and across different places and cultures, its history is generally characterized by marginalization and oppression. In the past, most societies have viewed disability through moral or medical models, perceiving it as a punishment, disease, tragedy, or misfortune. While on the surface, these views may appear distant, they remain prevalent in today's world.[8] Accessibility is only a recent chapter of a long and difficult journey.

For many reasons, disability has commonly been hidden or ridiculed. Places like Dime Museums, which were the first to link museums with disabilities, did so by encouraging curious and even morbid gazes or even by fomenting the audience's pity. The best known and most popular of these museums, both now and then, was what P. T. Barnum called the American Museum: a rich entertainment offering based in New York that included, among its attractions, a freak show that exhibited people with different physical and cognitive disabilities (so-called freaks) for the enjoyment of visitors. Dime Museums were popular for several decades at the turn of the twentieth century both in the United States and in Europe, and in some contexts, these profit-driven shows continue to inform exhibits and museum policies to this day.[9] These places were not museums in the traditional sense of the word, but freak shows and museums share a common trend of exhibiting the strange and the exceptional to a paying public.[10] The history of freak shows remains an uncomfortable and unresolved heritage. A study on these issues conducted by the University of Leicester reveals how in the UK, for example, this past often remains unaddressed and has even been rarely reproposed by museums. This story remains somewhat of a secret and raises a degree of compunction.[11]

During much of the last century, the perception of people with disabilities in the Western countries was rather negative, and discrimination was widespread: People were deprived of their freedom, confined to ghettos, and subjected to com-

Chapter 1

pulsory medical treatment. Contemporaneously, more actions were being taken in support of their rights, although sporadically. These interventions ranged from the contribution of charities and philanthropic organizations to the work of well-known figures like Louis Braille in France and later Helen Keller in the United States. In countries like Italy, the Catholic Church played a particularly significant role in spreading solidarity, yet its intervention often took on a patronizing tone. Some researchers believe this approach involuntarily hindered the development of disability studies in this country till today.[12]

According to Simon Hayhoe, some approaches in art education for blind people may go back as far as two hundred years and find their roots in religious beliefs and morality.[13] In parallel, the first initiatives to promote museum accessibility took place largely through tours and classes at natural history collections in England and New York.[14] One of the earliest records attesting to museum accessibility dates back to 1908 at the Metropolitan Museum of Art, where archival evidence indicates that visitors were able to borrow a chair to visit the museum, and hence gain better access to the collections.[15] In addition, the May 1913 "Bulletin of the Metropolitan Museum of Art" recounts the experience of two lectures given to blind visitors, while the first reference to "lectures for the deaf" were held a few years later in 1917.[16]

A history of museum accessibility has yet to be written, but records make it clear that museums inevitably held up a mirror to their times, reflecting both their contradictions and their social battles. When movements in defense of civil rights emerged, museums also began to make concerted efforts to facilitate accessibility:[17] They defined a new, though shaky, trend in the 1960s and 1970s that was recognized in museum studies shortly thereafter.[18]

Various activists, supporters, and organizations (mostly made up of people with disabilities and not only their supporters) waged battles founded on principles that are still valid for cultural institutions today. Hence this community forged the motto "Nothing about us without us" in opposition to paternalism and pietism and in support of autonomy and their right to rights. At the time, important campaigns made equally significant contributions to access regarding housing, education, work, and other fundamental issues. In the United States, for example, Nixon signed Section 504 of the Rehabilitation Act in 1973, prohibiting discrimination for the first time ever. The American Coalition of Citizens with Disabilities, the first disability rights group governed by disabled individuals, was created in 1975. That same year, the General Assembly of the United Nations signed "The Declaration on the Rights of Disabled Persons" which, together with "The Declaration on the Rights of Mentally Retarded Persons" (1971), was one of the first UN resolutions to specifically address people with disabilities.

Over the years, a new mentality aimed at supporting inclusion has also been cultivated by adopting laws requiring compliance with minimum standards of accessibility. Although they are clearly insufficient in and of themselves, it appears that such measures have helped in the diffusion of a new social awareness, first in the United States, then in the UK and in most of the countries of the world.

Nowadays, researchers like Catherine Kudlick and Edward Luby see the museum field as one of the many battlefields on which to pursue an activist agenda oriented by principles of social justice, including, but not limited to, the issue of disability.[19] The approaches may be very different, but for the most part there are shared objectives aimed at inclusion. We are still a long way from achieving this, but we are certainly in the midst of a process of transformation: It is now a matter of understanding how to make this truly effective, free from rhetoric and bias, and capable of generating a positive impact in people's lives.

DISABILITY STUDIES AND MODELS OF DISABILITIES

In 2020, it is estimated that more than one billion people live with some form of disability. This corresponds to 15 percent of the world's population, a figure that will inevitably increase as the population of some countries ages.[20] Referred to as "the third nation in the world,"[21] this group is not homogeneous and probably not even a minority: Disability may be severe or moderate, permanent or temporary, and may or may not cause physical and mental pain; it can include sensory, intellectual, or motor impairments or include several of these components. From heart disease to visual impairments, the boundaries that can be attributed to this condition are sometimes very nuanced. Disability is usually characterized by a diagnosis that merely frames the impairment. Diagnosis can be perceived as a label, but it is also a factor on which provisions of funds and support often rely. While some researchers define *disability* as a marker of identity, it is also important to mention that not everyone with a disability identifies themself with it. What is certain is that any reference to the condition remains fluid, as "anyone can enter [it] at any time, and we will all join it if we live long enough."[22] In fact, disabilities can occur at any time or stage of life and are especially common in old age.

These initial considerations underline the complexity of a theme that is anything but easy to frame: Disability is also a condition that is socially constructed and that—much like accessibility—requires understanding and analysis, especially on a cultural and political level. From this point of view, disability studies is a field that began to make its way in the 1970s, contributing to the construction of a (mostly academic) path that became increasingly rooted also in the civic and institutional fronts. The disability rights movements marked a decisive historical turning point by virtue of their conjunction with the development of *disability studies*, a research area that presents disability from a sociocultural perspective. This broad branch of studies, mainly developed in English-speaking countries and later in Northern Europe, has often furnished ideas for interdisciplinary and operational investigations in other fields (from education to sociology and law), although it seems to be examined only rarely in relation to museum studies.

The starting point for understanding these issues involves the development of a new framework that shifted the perception of disability from a medical model (prevalent until the twentieth century) to a social one, and now defines *disability* in function of a given context. This social model, formulated in the United Kingdom, again during the seventies, allowed disability to be finally understood as a condition that is also a product of environment and society for the first time, rather than an impairment that remains an exclusive attribute of an individual who may require treatment. Founded on the principles developed by the Union of the Physically Impaired Against Segregation (UPIAS), the social model was later theorized by so-ciologist Mike Oliver in 1983.[23] He defined a crucial approach—"the big idea"—for the disability rights movement in which *removing barriers* became a clear political strategy and allowed people with disabilities to understand that their condition was not their responsibility.[24] For this reason, this social model favors the term *disabled* as opposed to "people with disabilities" precisely because this renders the disabling role of the context explicit.

Over the years, the social model has inspired new approaches and theories, while becoming the object of criticism, especially from those who have accused it of a progressive stiffening with a narrowed focus on environmental factors. For researchers and activists like Tom Shakespeare, however, it is not just a matter of simplifying the distinction between medical and social models, but more generally between reductionist and multifactorial explanations.[25] One example involving the latter type is the biopsychosocial model, which emphasizes the complexity of disability by insisting on a multifactorial approach that incorporates both the medical and social models, looking at the dynamic interconnection between bio-logical, psychological, and social factors. This approach has also found a normative frame of reference in the International Classification of Functioning, which is the most recent classification proposed by the World Health Organization.[26] While all the social models insist on highlighting how essential it is to remove barriers to museums, the biopsychosocial model confirms this approach but also reminds us that, in the case of impairments, the removal of barriers does not always constitute a removal of the disability since it is outside the scope of the museum to act on this level. The latter approach is therefore, also, an invitation to consider intrinsic limitations alongside the context, offering critical insights for a questioning around the cases, for example, related to the inclusion at the museum of all those people who, even in an accessible space, might not find the museum welcoming, as in the case of people with severe intellectual disabilities. Overall, there is an important correlation between disability studies and accessibility, made evident, even in the last few years, in the emancipatory intentions of critical disability studies; the issues that emerge from this area of research must lie at the foundation for any institutional decision related to access.

THE IMPACT OF LEGISLATION

Normative achievements represent another fundamental step in recounting the development of accessibility as well as incongruities that have characterized the discipline's evolution in a variety of geographical contexts. As mentioned earlier, differences in cultural and political awareness have allowed accessibility to assume different forms around the world. In some countries, the social battles demanding greater equality and justice for people with disabilities have succeeded in defining regulations that ensure respect for the fundamental rights on a global scale and allow people to access employment and state and local services like transportation and communications. In this regard, a major benchmark for the discipline lies in the existence of laws that protect people with disabilities from discrimination and allow their participation in cultural activities.

While the "United Nations Year of People with a Disability" in 1982 was lauded internationally as a "landmark for the cultural accessibility of people with disabilities,"[27] years passed before we saw the emergence of structured legislations that granted a greater development of the discipline in some parts of the world. For instance, the United States and the UK advanced laws that provide historical precedents. Both countries had already adopted measures that were later supported by further legislation, namely the Americans with Disabilities Act (ADA) passed in 1990 and the Disability Discrimination Act of 1995.

These two regulatory systems represent best practices and are often cited as models capable of accompanying hundreds of institutions step by step in the definition of their own practices that might not otherwise have been fulfilled. In particular, the ADA represents a much-celebrated law that has had a very profound impact on museum activities and services geared toward people with disabilities. For many, it is not just a law but a veritable statement of intent on accessibility. Many widely used best practices are still in use today because of the support of this legislation. In addition, the ADA has also trained recipient museums to help them implement a whole range of facilities. Yet "Equality in theory does not mean equality in practice," as stated in an article by *Time* magazine celebrating the act's thirtieth anniversary.[28] Despite its many good intentions, there are many unsolved issues: Accessibility has not been achieved in many places just yet; access to employment is not guaranteed, nor is access to housing; and prisons are rarely able to meet the needs of people with disabilities, in addition to other injustices.[29] While this is noticeable in the United States, elsewhere in the world it is even more evident.

In the cultural field, it is also worth noting that a well-structured regulatory pathway has offered the opportunity to accompany the development of cutting-edge examples. It has, however, led to some minor challenges that are also worth mentioning due to indirect effects. On the one hand, these norms offer clear support to disciplinary diffusion as a "powerful engine for change," ensuring guidance for cultural institutions and obliging them to take appropriate measures.[30] On the other hand, some laws limit their autonomous development, leaving ample room for interpretation and implicitly suggesting that sometimes compliance with minimum standards may suffice. A careful analysis of Smith et al., for example, suggests that the very regulations that seem to structure solutions that facilitate access can also prove ambiguous and fail to spur institutions to dialogue with the people who are the objects of given accessibility solutions.[31]

In other countries, the situation is far more uncertain, as shown in Simon Prideaux's study for the Centre for Disability Studies at the University of Leeds.[32] The report analyzes six European countries and their provisions on physical access only. It reveals how, in some cases, normativity is subject to contextual variables that can take absolute priority and undermine the removal of barriers.

Given these premises, it is easy to understand how the adoption of accessibility practices, in compliance with normative regulations, proves more effective in providing guidance in overcoming *physical barriers*, while it is less successful regarding access to *content* or *history and culture* (following a distinction made in 1998 by Janice Majewski and Lonnie Bunch).[33] The removal of physical barriers can, in fact, be more easily achieved through the adoption of standard solutions. In other words, legislation has a powerful impact on the development of accessibility, although it often remains understood as a set of rules that do not facilitate an inclusive mindset. In their reference book on universal design, Edward Steinfeld and Jordana Maisel write how this kind of thinking can generate further misconceptions like the idea that disability needs can only be addressed through regulations.[34] In turn, this thought generates the false belief that these issues constitute a "problem for a small group of specialists to solve rather than an opportunity for creative design."[35] As always, exceptions must be made. For example, solutions that are popular in the United States, such as large print or even the adoption of standards for exhibition display elsewhere, are not always guaranteed. This tendency substantially determines the way in which institutions approach the subject, so much so that in nations where such legislation is less stringent, for reasons of cost and risk containment, it is easier to address the issue mostly through unstructured interventions that leave visitors wanting. Hence, legal norms are of absolute importance and concretely impact institutions. What is certain is that any proposals aimed merely at the fulfillment of standards are insufficient. To avoid this risk, it is necessary to assume a deep, shared meaning of this subject, while promoting an urgent understanding of its complexity.

NOTES

1. John P. S. Salmen, *Everyone's Welcome: The Americans with Disabilities Act and Museums* (Washington, DC: American Alliance of Museums, 1998), 3, https://files.eric.ed.gov/fulltext/ED437754.pdf.
2. "Definitions of Diversity, Equity, Accessibility, and Inclusion," American Alliance of Museums, accessed April 2, 2021, https://www.aam-us.org/programs/diversity-equity-accessibility-and-inclusion/facing-change-definitions/.

3. Helen Graham, "Museums and How to Know about Access," *New Formations*, no. 79 (Autumn 2013), 64, https://www.academia.edu/7754903/Museums_and_How_to_Know_About_Access.
4. Kat Holmes, *Mismatch: How Inclusion Shapes Design* (Cambridge: The MIT Press, 2020), 55.
5. Stephen E. Weil, "From Being about Something to Being for Somebody: The Ongoing Transformation of the American Museum," *Daedalus* 128, no. 3 (1999), accessed July 11, 2021, http://www.jstor.org/stable/20027573.
6. Gail Anderson, *Reinventing the Museum: The Evolving Conversation on the Paradigm Shift*, 2nd ed. (Lanham, MD: Alta Mira Press, 2012); Louise Roberts, *From Knowledge to Narrative: Educators and the Changing Museum* (Washington, DC: Smithsonian Institution Press, 1997).
7. John Kinard, "The Museum in the Service of Man Today and Tomorrow," in *Paper from the Ninth General Conference of ICOM*, 151–156, Paris, ICOM, 1972.
8. Dan Goodley, *Disability Studies: An Interdisciplinary Introduction*, 2nd ed. (Thousand Oaks, CA: SAGE, 2017), Kindle.
9. Katie Stringer, "The Legacy of Dime Museums and the Freakshow: How the Past Impacts the Present," *American Association for State and Local History*, Autumn 2013, accessed February 23, 2021, https://aaslh.org/the-legacy-of-dime-museums-and-the-freakshow-how-the-past-impacts-the-present/.
10. Katie Stringer, "Disability, the Sideshow, and Modern Museum Practices," *Scientia et Humanitas* 3 (2013), https://libjournals.mtsu.edu/index.php/scientia/article/view/551.
11. Richard Sandell and Annie Delin, "In the Shadow of the Freakshow: The Impact of Freakshow Tradition on the Display and Understanding of Disability History in Museums," *Disability Studies Quarterly*, 4, no. 25 (Fall 2005), https://dsq-sds.org/article/view/614/791.
12. Simona D'Alessio, "Disability Studies in Education: Implicazioni per la ricerca educativa e la pratica scolastica italiana," in *Disability Studies, Emancipazione, inclusione scolastica e sociale, cittadinanza*, ed. Roberto Medeghini et al. (Trento: Erickson, 2013).
13. Simon Hayhoe, *Blind Visitor Experiences at Art Museums* (New York: Rowman & Littlefield, 2017).
14. Ibid.
15. Tanya Mohn, "Welcoming Art Lovers with Disabilities," *New York Times*, October 25, 2013, accessed January 12, 2021, https://www.nytimes.com/2013/10/27/arts/artsspecial/welcoming-art-lovers-with-disabilities.html.
16. "Bulletin of the Metropolitan Museum of Art," 8, no. 5 (1913). The author gathered this information in 2014 directly at the Metropolitan Museum while consulting photocopies of original documents whose references are now difficult to recover.
17. "ADA | Maintaining Accessibility in Museums," U.S. Department of Justice, Civil Rights Division, accessed April 21, 2021, www.ada.gov/business/museum_access.htm.
18. Graham Black, *The Engaging Museum: Developing Museums for Visitor Involvement* (London: Routledge, 2005); Peter Van Mensch and Léontine Meijer-Van Mensch, *New Trends in Museology* (Celje, Slovenia: Celje Museum of Recent History, 2011).

19. Catherine Kudlick and Edward M. Luby, "Access as Activism: Bringing the Museum to the People," in *Museum Activism*, ed. Robert R. Janes and Richard Sandell (London: Routledge, 2019).
20. "Disability and Health," World Health Organization, accessed March 21, 2021, https://www.who.int/news-room/fact-sheets/detail/disability-and-health.
21. Matteo Schianchi, *La terza nazione del mondo: I disabili tra pregiudizio e realtà* (Feltrinelli: Milano, 2009).
22. Rosemarie Garland-Thomson, "Integrating Disability, Transforming Feminist Theory," *NWSA Journal*, 14, no. 3 (2002), 20, https://www.jstor.org/stable/4316922?-origin=JSTOR-pdf.
23. Nick Watson and Simo Vehmas, *Routledge Handbook of Disability Studies*, 2nd ed. (Abingdon, OX: Routledge, 2020).
24. Tom Shakespeare, *Disabilità e società: Diritti, falsi miti, percezioni sociali* (Trento: Erikson, 2017).
25. Ibid.
26. The International Classification of Functioning (ICF) was officially endorsed as the international standard to describe and measure health and disability by all 191 member states of the World Health Organization at the 54th World Health Assembly on May 22, 2001.
27. Marcus Weisen, *International Perspectives on the Cultural Accessibility of People with Disabilities: A Project Access White Paper* (New York: Art Beyond Sight, 2012), 1. http://www.artbeyondsight.org/mei/wp-content/uploads/WP_International_Perspectives-REV.pdf.
28. Abigail Abrams, "30 Years after a Landmark Disability Law, the Fight for Access and Equality Continues," *Time*, July 23, 2020, accessed May 13, 2021, https://time.com/5870468/americans-with-disabilities-act-coronavirus/.
29. Ibid.
30. Heather J. L. Smith, Barry Gingley, and Hanna Goodwin, "Beyond Compliance? Museums, Disability and the Law," in *Museums, Equality and Social Justice*, ed. Richard Sandell and Eithne Nightingale (London: Routledge, 2012).
31. Ibid.
32. Ibid., 62.
33. Janice Majewski and Lonnie Bunch, "The Expanding Definition of Diversity: Accessibility and Disability Culture Issues in Museum Exhibitions," *Curator* 41, no. 3 (1998), https://doi.org/10.1111/j.2151-6952.1998.tb00829.x.
34. Edward Steinfeld and Jordana Maisel, *Universal Design: Creating Inclusive Environments* (Hoboken, NJ: Wiley, 2012).
35. Ibid., 68.

2

Accessibility as a Visitor-Oriented Process

The investigation of museums as spaces of encounter and mediation with visitors is a vast domain through which to discuss accessibility. Commonly, researching the physicality of a place leads us mainly to consider the needs of those who pass through it, perhaps in a wheelchair, although the factors to be taken into account are much more numerous and more often cognitive in nature.

The starting point for understanding its complexity is to identify with the visitors who generally consider the museum as an authoritative space. Both empirical evidence and recent research, in fact, suggest that visitors traditionally trust museums.[1] Proof of this trust can be found in the misbelief that any visitors' difficulties are their responsibilities due to their own lack of attention, skills, or knowledge. Rarely does one implicate the museum in its failure to create fully accessible spaces. The case, of course, is different for people with disabilities, who are used to encountering barriers and recognize them immediately—although even this tendency varies greatly based on personal experience and from country to country.

More generally, when moving through galleries or other museum spaces, people rely primarily on content without realizing that the museum's choices regarding mediation, education, and accessibility implicitly influence them; at the same time, museums believe they have fulfilled their duty by adopting minimal guidelines that ensure access for people with disabilities. This double paradox is one of the main ones that characterizes accessibility.

We see a similar situation in education, an area that partially overlaps with access. Both disciplines are geared toward reaching a wider audience by facilitating access to content. Moreover, both accessibility and education are kept at a clear distance from curatorship and other exhibition functions, so much so that it has been said that "the museum curatorially constructs the mystery that its education function must then solve for the audience."[2]

There is a significant gap between areas that cater to audiences (such as education and accessibility) and those that do so indirectly (like curatorship or design exhibition), resulting in a fragmented system that often conveys conflicting messages to audiences, something that visitors are not always able to grasp. Greater collaboration between these areas could generate new opportunities regarding not only the full adoption of accessibility standards but also questions of interpretation, relations between spatial layout and cognitive motivation, reflections on visitors' attention spans, and the orientation of exhibition spaces. These issues—often considered marginal—are valid for every type of museum but are rarely addressed in literature dedicated to accessibility.

To home in on this disparity, we need to look at institutions that are considered to be at the forefront of education and accessibility for people with disabilities but that, unreasonably, offer an inaccessible visitor experience to the general public through confusing exhibition layouts, illegible captions, and poorly trained staff. It is interesting to note that many museums overlook familiar issues like the lack of adequate seating or the use of poorly contrasted captions and, for example, show more concern about adding braille text even though it may not necessarily be the most urgent or effective solution. All these elements allow us, as professionals, to perceive the enormous difficulties we are up against in terms of access and grasp the resounding absence of a broad and holistic vision.

To bridge this disjuncture, it is often said that the strategies aimed at addressing the needs of people with disabilities are, in fact, beneficial to all visitors. Though this view is often true, it is rarely useful in terms of redefining perceptions of the discipline or its widespread application. Claiming that traditional accessibility is advantageous to all can just perpetuate the idea that for many, it provides only an added benefit, rather than recognizing its substantial value. What rarely emerges from these reflections is just how essential accessibility is to everyone—in different ways and for different purposes—across the board. Moreover, it is often impossible to establish a clear demarcation *a priori* between what must or must not be deemed accessible, especially if we think of cultural barriers. In addition, the distinction between those who need support and those who do not can be blurry and change over time.

When defining the essential constraints of any design, accessibility offers fundamental criteria; if considered only in hindsight, it remains a missed opportunity. For this reason, accessibility must be framed in a broader and more multifaceted context—not just on the educational or architectural front. In order to ensure they are offering the highest quality experience, museums must make sure that as many people as possible can embark on an autonomous visit, also thinking of those who are not flexible in their organization, or even tourists. Of course, insisting on autonomy will not be equally meaningful for those who need an experience based on relation (such as visitors with dementia), but more generally it would allow people to scratch the surface of the museum and demonstrate the importance assigned to accessibility. Contrary to popular belief, this would often mean designing an experience that is also for the full benefit of people with disabilities. In all cases, what needs to be changed is the overall paradigm: The needs this discipline addresses are never special needs. In fact, it makes a significant difference when we consider them entirely normal, as explained in further detail below.

EVERY EXPERIENCE IS COMPLEX

To understand the complexity of museums, we need to observe the various phenomena that shape them, investigate the cognitive variables at play, and strive for a wider understanding of their spaces as multilayered and rich in stimuli, distractions, and messages (coherent or discordant as they may be). A multiplicity of factors, which are only rarely taken into consideration, shine light on their articulate nature. Tiina Roppola invites us to recalibrate our perception by considering the intricacy of our own museum experience, one made up of overlapping elements, including "how you engaged with an exhibit after exhibit through various combinations of sight, sound and touch; how you felt stimulated, entranced, distracted, weary; how you judged something as being real or authentic; how you experienced states of remembering, knowing and familiarity; how you 'read' and responded to the architecture of the building as you navigated your way through exhibition spaces."[3] Museums are places where visitors can feel assailed by doubts and questions. As Tom Hennes puts it, "The visitor is the one who initiates the experience itself, becoming an active explorer, a problem solver seeking an answer."[4] Yet not all visitors feel at ease with all these roles in this environment.

In essence, museums can generate a sense of disquiet in some people, a feeling that is best resolved before it morphs into frustration. There has not been any significant increase in the awareness of the complexity—especially cognitive—of museum spaces despite the growing theoretical attention paid toward the public in recent years. Similarly, the idea of facilitating the visitor experience through a more holistic approach has been left relatively unexplored, as has most discourse about the professional skills that such facilitation would involve. By straddling accessibility, usability, and quality of experience, museums can avoid unnecessary struggle and dissatisfaction and find solutions through the process of facilitating a visitor's path.

Approaching a human-centered model requires a change of perspective, analyzing the implications of a visit from a variety of viewpoints and refocusing the investigation of what is generically defined as the "museum experience." The Contextual Model of Learning, developed by John Falk and Lynn Dierking, offers perhaps one of the best-known frameworks for understanding this experience.[5] This model, in which learning has an inescapable role, presents the visitor with experience according to three main variables: personal, social, and contextual factors. Personal factors include all individual attributes like motivation, interest, previous experience, gender, age, ability, and any other characteristics that define the person. On the other hand, sociocultural factors are an unavoidable result of human interactions and take into account learning experiences that inevitably stem from a given social and cultural environment. Lastly, contextual factors involve those relating to the physical space in which an experience takes shape; they include the setting and architectural space, as well as elements like exhibits and the museum's communication tools.

These factors overlap to shape an experience that is unique to each individual visit. What's more, a context's inaccessibility is relative to the specific set of circumstances at play. Consider, for example, how the degree of access can change radically for some visitors depending on whether they see a museum alone or with a companion. Clearly, this sort of relative accessibility is not true in all situations: A flight of stairs makes wheelchair access completely impracticable whether accompanied or not.

When conducting a practical investigation of the museum experience, it is essential to pay close attention to the timeline of the visit, from beginning to end, examining all the obstacles and challenges that the process may entail. Just think of the braille labels cited above: If we do not establish pathways that support visitor autonomy from the entrance to the exhibit, we are assuming that people will be accompanied by someone else. In that case, it might be easier—at least from a logistical point of view—to provide audio content or even proposals able to prompt conversation. In other words, analyzing the path according to this logic always provides us with additional information: For many scholars, the experience begins not at the time of arrival, but with the moment of choice, meaning that an analysis of the experience must also include, for example, the website used by the visitor before the visit itself.

It is this approach that underpins the interdisciplinary title "Museum Thresholds," which examines the specificities and significance of the museum atrium.[6] This highly symbolic space is uniquely positioned to function as a declaration of intent; this purpose extends to the field of accessibility, as it is here that we see how visitors are welcomed, what tools and services are made available, as well as the museum's ability to communicate its competence in this area. It is, therefore, a matter of responding to visitor needs and expectations from the outset, not just in terms of the resources provided, but through the way in which these solutions are presented, such as facilitating orientation, explaining the support tools available, and making sure they are not disregarded at a later stage.

Essential access needs (physical, sensorial, and intellectual) must, of course, be taken into account, as well as cultural, relational, and emotional requirements of a cross-cutting nature. The "Visitors' Bill of Rights" drawn up by the Visitor Services Association in 2001 offers a clear outline of the different needs that arise throughout the various stages of the visit:

- Comfort: "Meet my basic needs."
- Orientation: "Make it easy for me to find my way around."
- Welcome/belonging: "Make me feel welcome."

- Enjoyment: "I want to have fun."
- Socializing: "I came to spend time with my family and friends."
- Respect: "Accept me for who I am and what I know."
- Communication: "Help me understand and let me talk too."
- Learning: "I want to learn something new."
- Choice and control: "Let me choose; give me some control."
- Challenge and confidence: "Give me a challenge I know I can handle."
- Revitalization: "Help me leave refreshed, restored."[7]

Owing to its seemingly obvious nature, the value of this list has often been underestimated, yet if we comply with its tenets and define appropriate strategies to fulfill them, then its aims represent a fundamental contribution toward achieving accessibility. Graham Black, mentioning this list, highlights aspects of the visitor experience that determine the quality of welcome, involvement, and well-being offered by the museum, elements whose value must be on a par with a more traditional concept of accessibility.[8]

BEHAVIORAL NUDGES

Visitors are expected to walk slowly in a museum, to pause, observe an object or artifact, listen to the audio guide or read the caption carefully, to learn something, leave good feedback, and possibly return. In other words, there are high expectations with regard to the mode of visiting, starting from the assumption that recipients of the museum experience are presumed to be similar to their designers, an error that occurs so frequently as to appear inevitable. As if this were not enough, the museum environment often provides counterintuitive directions that fail to indicate what behavior is expected of everyday visitors. For example, will someone with a general interest in a topic really watch or listen to a ten-minute video if they can't find a place to sit down? Is it reasonable to imagine that visitors will linger over a succession of apparently identical objects if they are not provided with a pretext or an explanation of the selection? These topics are rarely investigated by museums, partly because the most widely used evaluation tools inadequately describe and measure a visitor's experience. While experts engaged in the digital transformation are active in the widespread discussion of neuroscience, cognitive bias, and behavior, there is a lack of educational opportunities in these areas for museum professionals.

In this regard, it may be fruitful to recontextualize the opportunities presented by the concept of behavioral nudges, as described by economists Richard Thaler and Cass Sunstein in 2008.[9] According to Thaler and Sunstein, it is possible to exert a subtle influence over people's behavior by means of simple interventions that are beneficial to the recipients, while preserving their freedom of choice. What we need is to devise solutions that provide a cognitive nudge that goads people to do what is suggested to them precisely because it is designed for their own benefit: For example, an easy-to-read and well-visible label is certainly more appealing to read than a hidden, small, incomprehensible one. The founding premise of these gentle nudges is part of an important body of research within the field of social sciences, conducted with the aim of understanding cognitive biases and heuristics—i.e., constructs based on automatic ways of thinking and biases that enable decision-making. As yet there is not enough literature on the application of this concept within the museum world, but it is fair to assume that many of the solutions that insist on accessibility and involvement strategies could be informed by these modalities, offering a predictable yet unobtrusive means of positively conditioning the actions performed within the museum. Persuasive design, as it is called in other fields, could provide a wide range of solutions to issues like posting clear directions, facilitating visitor flow, or avoiding information overload. This transferrable principle surely deserves further investigation and experimentation, even on the smallest scales.

Looking further at nudges, we also need to consider the role of usability in changing habits. Defined as the use of a service or tool making it "easy to use, easy to learn, easy to remember, and useful to users," usability makes an unequivocal contribution to cognitive ergonomics, rendering the experience more approachable. This concept, most frequently associated with the digital realm, can also find ample scope in the context of a physical environment. When used in reference to accessibility, the term *usability* carries significant ambiguity, even within the research field, but there is a general tendency to regard usability as an approach that improves the user experience for anyone, while accessibility is solely for the benefit of people with disabilities. That said, the two concepts continue to be closely related. More specifically, usability provides some methodological guidance that will also be explored in this volume, for example, in the process of prototyping. Yet for now it is important to note that usability is often also a perceptual characteristic, with the aesthetic-usability bias serving as an invitation to design tools that appeal as much as possible to the outside world. To put it another way, the more aesthetically appealing an object or service, the easier we think it will be to use. Usability therefore serves as a positive driver of our attention, in line with the designer's presumed aspirations.

SUPPORTING ATTENTION

A visitor's attention is crucial to the quality of their experience. Although there are certain exceptions (particularly on a social and relational level), a distracted visitor is unlikely to fully appreciate their museum experience. This issue is somewhat self-perpetuating and depends on a variety of personal and environmental factors. On the personal side, we cannot ignore the importance of interest and intrinsic motivation, as we will see shortly. The environment, on the other hand, needs to employ strategies that do not exceed people's attention span before the visit is over.

In fact, attention is a rather inflexible resource with well-defined limits. Authors including Beverly Serrell and John Veverka remind us that too much information, for instance, can be counterproductive, as well as inaccessible for many target audiences.[10] One culprit in the issue of museum fatigue is mere overload, which is sometimes referred to as workload (of time and effort); it is not limited to consuming information in text or audio form, since excessively long paths and a lack of variety further contribute to the problem. The concept of information overload has been freshly reconsidered in recent years as a result of the constant digital stimulation to which we are subjected. Tiina Roppola brings our attention to Alt and Shaw's findings dating back to the eighties, studies reporting that even the most interactive environment can cause fatigue.[11] This becomes apparent to us when we visit museums that heavily lean on installations, as is often the case in scientific institutions. Being exposed to an overwhelming array of stimuli is likely to result in premature feelings of tiredness. Curiosity pushes us to explore such installations in rapid succession, one after the other, making it difficult to concentrate. Back in 1916, Benjamin Gilman was the first to explore the idea of museum fatigue in his study dedicated to demands placed on visitors in relation to exhibition design.[12] He used photographs to illustrate the absurdity of the poses sometimes assumed by visitors when reading captions placed in uncomfortable locations.

Numerous studies have identified that the real challenge for the twenty-first century is to compete for attention, and this is no less true of museums. Psychologist Stephen Bitgood has perhaps conducted the most thorough investigation of this issue in the museum context, defining the three key principles that govern our attention.[13] The first, which we have already discussed, is its limited capacity, but selectivity and motivation are also decisive elements. It is interesting to note that to the same author's principle to "minimize perceived effort" (or distractions), the solutions implemented partially overlap with those that are typically employed to improve cognitive accessibility.[14] To take again the example of a caption, a detailed design around it does not guarantee its being read. Numerous empirical factors influence the visitor when deciding whether to read it or not, which could be related to its formal style, but also meaning, understandability, the habits of the reader, their interest in the topic, and many more.

Nevertheless, in the attempt to preserve visitor attention, it is important to avoid oversimplifying content. Unnecessary effort should, therefore, be reduced while posing a challenge appropriate for a variety of abilities, planning different strategies accordingly. Trivializing the visitor experience by rendering it excessively easy can have the unintended effect of lowering the threshold of involvement. The goal is to create an accessible experience without limiting the component of (cognitive) challenge, which remains, for every visitor, a vital element. We find a clear expression of this kind of challenge in the concept of flow theory introduced in the seventies by Mihaly Csikszentmihalyi, which describes a state in which people are attentive because they are fully immersed in the flow of a rewarding activity.[15] According to this scholar, this state of flow occurs when there is an adequate balance between the level of difficulty and the person's abilities, whatever they might be. Anxiety and frustration emerge when difficulties outweigh relatively low skill levels, while boredom results when one possesses skills that easily overcome a given challenge. The key requisites for activating flow state include clear goals and appropriate rules. Unclear expectations and vague goals cause attention to wander, as does a lack of feedback and intrinsic motivation. Intrinsic and extrinsic motivation clearly derive from differing sets of prerequisites. Museums depend much more on elements of the former, such as personal interest and curiosity. In this sense, loyal audiences often fall into the umbrella of "non-captive audiences": They are present of their own volition, leisure-based, motivated from within, and for this reason, more likely to be attentive to a museum's proposals.[16]

Deborah Perry also believes that visitors do not perform an action without conditions that generate the intrinsic motivation for them to do so.[17] Perry's educational theoretical framework, which is applicable to all aspects of the museum experience, proposes a tripartite perspective of complementary elements that contribute to the effectiveness of the visit: outcomes (i.e., what visitors will get at the end of the visit), engagement, and motivation. Once again, the assumption is that audience involvement should be as cognitively active as possible, a conviction also shared by George E. Hein and Eilean Hooper-Greenhill, who view visitors always as active interpreters.[18] It is, therefore, necessary to solicit the construction of personal meaning in order to sustain motivation, prompting museums to move away from a linear model based on knowledge transfer to a multifaceted, dialogic model that invites visitors to formulate personal opinions and implies interaction.

MULTIMODAL APPROACHES TO LEARNING

Another way to solicit attention and promote accessibility is to differentiate the strategies for approaching the visit. Exhibition spaces benefit most when they are designed to maintain good levels of attention in order to accompany recipients throughout their visit, providing them with a constant source of fresh motivation (alternated with moments of rest), which they can experience at their own pace.

There is an open and sometimes controversial debate around visitors and their preferred learning styles; this lens offers a useful way to encourage a range of approaches to accessibility.[19] According to the *VARKT* model, introduced in 1992 by Neil D. Fleming and Colleen Mills, there are four main learning styles: *Visual, Auditory, Read/write,* and *KinesThetic.*[20] This method originally set out to find a match between visitor preferences and the options available in the exhibition. While the idea of differentiating approaches to learning has found many supporters over the years, its application has remained sporadic. Today, choices tend to be oriented toward multilayered displays "containing a combination of media [that potentially] hold the most appeal for visitors" as they present a variety of opportunities that cater to different modes of learning.[21] On the need to "combat museum fatigue," Graham Black suggests an "experiential matrix" in which different rooms address different purposes, enabling visitors to become involved through a variety of modes: contemplative, participatory, immersive, aesthetic, contributory, and in a seated reflection zone.[22]

The driving principle behind these considerations is that there are limits to sustained attention, and the introduction of new approaches throughout the itinerary provides visitors with opportunities to reactivate their engagement. In recent years, there have been mixed responses to diversified educational strategies, even within the spectrum of different museum types, yet museums have accepted the spread of multisensory modes of learning more widely. The result is that "the nonvisual senses are no longer regarded as simply second-rate ways of apprehending art for those who can't see, but rather as modalities through which anyone can receive meaningful and stimulating impressions."[23]

The relationship between the museum and the senses cannot be defined as linear, given that, like any other human experience, the visitor experience is, by its very nature, associated with multiple sensory strategies.[24] The sensory turn that seems to have taken shape in different fields, from contemporary art to marketing, is still far from established in the museum world, and the experiments underway are few and far between. The sensory hierarchy by which sight is accorded absolute preeminence has thus far proved difficult to undermine, though the benefits of a multisensory experience are evident in terms of the impact on memory, involvement, and, of course, accessibility.

What some define as sensory design is, in fact, a deeply inclusive approach that enhances the visitor experience by making content accessible via multiple strategies. At the same time, however, it is also useful to avoid unnecessary or even counterproductive overstimulation, even when recipients are people with sensory disabilities: It is a matter of evaluating on a case-by-case basis whether the coexistence of different stimuli makes access to content easier or more difficult.

With regard to this aspect, it is also important to make the distinction between multisensory experience and interaction, with the latter possible only when, as Steven Slack reminds us, the visitor is asked for an opinion, and not merely when they are called upon to smell something.[25] Engaging with the senses makes the museum experience more accessible, not only because it allows for the differentiation of access strategies, but also because it can offer different interpretive perspectives.

THE INTERSECTION BETWEEN ACCESS AND INTERPRETATION

Despite its correlation with educational activity, interpretation—as a mediation of possible meanings—is often neglected from the standpoint of accessibility. Yet, interpretation is a central function of the museum. This place, in fact, does not represent the world, but only offers possible interpretations of it: Spaces, objects, and ideas are ready to be expressed in different ways to reach different audiences. According to Freeman Tilden, one of the field's most recognized experts and the proponent of numerous principles[26] that remain valid across a range of disciplines, heritage interpretation must be considered "an educational activity whose purpose is to reveal messages and relationships through the use of original objects, through direct experience and illustrative tools, rather than to communicate factual information."[27]

Consequently, we can see the museum as a place that narrates itself by defining a series of interpretive filters, most explicitly in text or audio form: whether that means welcoming visitors with long introductions, adopting a white cube approach, using essential questions, providing captions or podcasts signed by the authors themselves, or utilizing those co-designed with visitors. Each of these choices can be associated with a precise value, revealing, however silently, the museum's awareness level and degree of orientation toward the public. Therefore, interpretation and the choices associated with it can either generate or impede access opportunities. Just consider the ineffectiveness of projects that attempt to address the needs of people with cognitive disabilities by only simplifying the wording, while failing to act on the content itself, maybe making it more familiar to life experience. The result is a set of captions and texts that are highly accessible on a formal level, but which remain strictly specialized in terms of content objectives. Visitors often do not have the tools to decode objects, with artworks being a prime example. There is growing demand for a range of interpretive registers to be made available that render content accessible to the broadest possible spectrum of people in terms of interest and existing skills. Of course, this does not mean that we should disregard history or specialist and disciplinary studies, but rather that we need to reach out to people who would not traditionally frequent such places.

When pondering the instrumental value of an object, we must remember that its narrative may be centered around any number of focal points, such as history, technical workmanship, the maker's biography, or the reasons for its belonging to a specific collection, to name just a few. More recently, there has even been a move toward exploiting an object's polysemous potential as a pretext to recount the present. By suggesting the use of counterstereotypes and minority voices in relation to dominant narratives, this approach responds to the same tendency that is driving museums toward increasingly inclusive and multivocal interpretive practices.

On this topic, Pat Villeneuve and Ann Rowson Love's analysis proves particularly insightful. It focuses on the number of interpretive opportunities while recognizing "the gap between the understanding of art by the general public and that of insiders, such as traditional museum experts."[28] They refer to Michael J. Parsons's 1989 study that defines five levels of aesthetic development (i.e., the different ways in which visitors spontaneously respond to a work of art). The analysis shows that those with a lower level of experience and awareness tend to respond to works of art in terms of their preferences with regard to recognizable elements such as color or subject (namely Favoritism). The second level is concerned with Beauty and Realism, and it is here that the general public largely falls, with most people observing the aesthetic quality of the subject depicted and the degree of realism. As the skill level increases, we progress to the group of people whose attention lands on what Parson calls Expression (relating to the emotions and feelings the work solicits), and then Style and Form, where the focus is more specifically on identifying connections to the art world. The final, and perhaps most interesting, level is defined as Autonomy. In this category, we find only the most experienced visitors, those able to analyze work from various perspectives and even consider it from different disciplinary standpoints.

This schematization proves useful in breaking down homogeneous approaches aimed exclusively at an ideal audience (for instance, following the level of Style and Form) but it also appears interesting in reference to the challenges posed by verbal description for blind users. Indeed, it is only at the final level, Autonomy, that it becomes possible to conceive of the work as a tool of open reflection, or even as an activator of a conversation around differentiated themes. This framework thus constitutes a useful reflection strategy, not only with regard to accessibility, but also in the move toward empowering different audiences in an experience that can be rewarding for all.

NOTES

1. Elizabeth Merritt, "Trust Me, I'm a Museum," *Centre for the Future of Museums Blog*, February 3, 2015, accessed February 1, 2021, https://www.aam-us.org/2015/02/03/trust-me-im-a-museum/.
2. Brian Hogart, "Rethinking Curator/Educator Training and Interaction in the Co-Production of Art Museum Exhibitions," in *Visitor-Centered Exhibitions and Edu-Curation in Art Museums*, ed. Pat Villeneuve and Ann Rowson Love (Lanham, MD: Rowman & Littlefield, 2017), loc. 604 of 5417, Kindle.
3. Tiina Roppola, *Designing for the Museum Visitor Experience* (New York: Routledge, 2011), loc. 1380–1385 of 8179, Kindle.
4. Tom Hennes, "Rethinking the Visitor Experience," *Curator: The Museum Journal* 45, no. 2 (2002), 115, https://doi.org/10.1111/cura.2002.45.issue-1.
5. John H. Falk and Lynn D. Dierking, *Learning from Museums: Visitor Experiences and the Making of Meaning* (Lanham, MD: AltaMira Press, 2020).
6. Ross Parry, Ruth Page, and Alex Moseley, *Museum Thresholds: The Design and Media of Arrival* (London: Routledge, 2020).
7. Judy Rand, "Visitors' Bill of Rights," in Roxana Adams, *Museums Visitor Service Manual* (Washington, DC: American Association of Museums, 2001), 13–14.
8. Graham Black, *Transforming Museums in the Twenty-First Century* (Abingdon, OX: Routledge, 2012).
9. Richard H. Thaler and Cass R. Sunstein, *Nudge: Improving Decisions about Health, Wealth and Happiness* (London: Penguin Books Ltd, 2008).
10. Beverly Serrell, *Exhibit Labels: An Interpretative Approach*, 2nd ed. (Lanham, MD: Rowman & Littlefield, 2015); John A. Veverka, *Interpretive Training Handbook: Content, Strategies, Tips, Handouts and Practical Learning Experiences for Teaching Interpretation to Others* (Edinburgh: MuseumsEtc, 2011).
11. Roppola, *Designing for the Visitor Experience*, loc. 569 of 8179, Kindle.
12. Benjamin Ives Gilman, "Museum Fatigue," *Scientific Monthly* 12 (1916), https://www.jstor.org/stable/6127?seq=1#metadata_info_tab_contents.

13. Stephen Bitgood, "The Role of Attention in Designing Effective Interpretive Labels," *Journal of Interpretation Research* 5, no. 2 (2003).
14. Ibid.
15. Mihaly Csikszentmihalyi, *Flow: The Psychology of Optimal Experience* (New York: Harper & Row, 1990).
16. Sam Ham, *Interpretation: Making a Difference on Purpose* (Golden, CO: Fulcrum Publishing, 2016).
17. Deborah Perry, *What Makes Learning Fun? Principles for the Design of Intrinsically Motivating Museum Exhibits* (Lanham, MD: Rowman Altamira, 2012).
18. George Hein, *Learning in the Museum* (Abingdon, OX: Routledge, 1998); Eilean Hooper-Greenhill, *Museum, Media, Message* (London: Routledge, 1999).
19. Roppola, *Designing for the Visitor Experience*, loc. 692 of 8179, Kindle.
20. Neil D. Fleming and Coleen E. Mills, "Not Another Inventory, Rather a Catalyst for Reflection," *To Improve the Academy* 11 (1992), https://doi.org/10.1002/j.2334-4822.1992.tb00213.x.
21. Roppola, *Designing for the Visitor Experience*, loc. 719 of 8179, Kindle.
22. Graham Black, *Museums and the Challenge of Change* (Abington, OX: Routledge, 2021), loc. 167 of 314, VitalSource Bookshelf.
23. Constance Classen, *The Museum of the Senses: Experiencing Art and Collections* (London: Bloomsbury Academic, 2017), 129.
24. Nina Levent and Alvaro Pascual-Leone, *The Multisensory Museum: Cross-Disciplinary Perspectives on Touch, Sounds, Smell, Memory, and Space* (Lanham, MD: Rowman & Littlefield, 2014), Kindle.
25. Steven Slack, *Interpreting Heritage: A Guide to Planning and Practice* (London: Routledge, 2021).
26. The so-called TIPs (Tilden's Interpretive Principles) were written in 1957 and are published in Freeman Tilden, *Practices for Visitor Services in Parks, Museums, and Historic Places* (Chapel Hill, NC: North Carolina Press, 2008). The principles are summarized by John A. Veverka, *The Interpretive Training Handbook* (Edinburgh: MuseumsEtc, 2011), 70–71: "1. All interpretive efforts should relate to the personality, experience, or interest of the visitor. 2. Information does not correspond to interpretation, but all interpretations contain information. 3. Interpretation is an art that combines different arts regardless of material subject matter. All art is teachable in some way. 4. Interpretation does not equate to instruction, but rather to provocation. 5. Interpretation should aim to present a whole rather than a part. 6. Interpretation for children should be designed specifically for children."
27. Freeman Tilden, *Interpreting Our Heritage*, 3rd ed. (Chapel Hill: University of North Carolina Press, 1977), 8.
28. Villeneuve and Rowson Love, *Visitor-Centered Exhibitions*, loc. 301 of 5417, Kindle.

3

All Visitors Need Access

The only way to build successful relationships with visitors and, more importantly, ensure their accessibility, is to understand them *a priori*. This means identifying who they are, what they want, and what kind of barriers they might find: insights that can only be achieved through research and evaluation involving theory and hands-on investigation. Studies of this kind are also essential when it comes to dismantling clichés and stereotypes, giving museums a new awareness of their visitors' characteristics and strengths. By thinking about their audiences in simplistic ways, museums are sometimes left stranded.

Despite the emergence of new categories of visitors over the years (like teenagers or the elderly), we are still looking at a relatively restricted number of clusters, often based on sociodemographic data. These serve best as guides for planning educational activities or for setting different entrance fees. More recently, we have also seen a growing focus on identity-based clusters in order to break down specific barriers and foster opportunities for representation of different social groups in terms of race, gender, sexuality, and many others. Disability often falls between such considerations. Although many believe, even correctly, that these strategies allow museums to set the right tone for their programs and be more inclusive, we also need to consider ways in which these elements might limit our ability to look at people from different perspectives, especially with regard to their interests and motivations, which can be more diverse than expected.

For a museum to develop an equitable relationship with its visitors, it must first recognize their active value, fluid opinions, and complex identities. Overly simplistic labeling prevents us from seeing visitors as "imaginative, autonomous, and self-directed" people capable of creating "meaning based on their worldview and social situation."[1] Accepting that audiences may diverge from what museums expect also means accepting visitors who reject the museum and its values as a challenge to face today.

AUDIENCES ARE ACTIVE

When considering adult visitors, we know that we cannot disregard their personal experience, whatever that may be. Indeed, the significance of personal factors, such as a visitor's existing knowledge and know-how, plays a substantial role in shaping each new visit experience, an aspect highlighted in the Falk and Dierking model cited in the previous chapter. Our experience of the world is always, inevitably framed by what we already know, think, and believe, which also applies to the museum environment. This means that visitors are actively engaged in the construction of meaning,[2] since what they observe is constantly compared with their own experience. In other words, it is clear that people are not merely empty vessels to be filled with information and that convincing them or imparting knowledge through purely transmissive means will always prove unsuccessful.

Yet, in the history of cultural and media studies, such considerations have not always been a given. This school of thought only began taking shape in the fifties and sixties, when it was established "that people expose themselves to understand and remember communication selectively according to prior dispositions."[3] Thus began our understanding of audiences, not as passive recipients of media, as with television *in primis*, but rather as active agents with the ability to negotiate meanings and contribute to their construction.

In the museum world, this awareness has a significant impact, since it requires every visitor to be viewed, regardless of their individual specificities, as a peer, not so much in terms of disciplinary expertise but in life experience. Accordingly, museums must find new modes of cultural communication that are not simply transmissive, but able to solicit autonomous reflections and harness the power of each person. These notions, which originated in the humanities, have since received support from educational theorists, who have reaffirmed the central role of meaning-making in museum learning.

This approach is based on the idea that visitors may no longer be willing to "learn" what a museum has in mind for them, but are always subjects who choose, negotiate, and even reject. Adopting this vision also helps to delegitimize the patronizing perspective of museums as bearers of truth, and foster a genuine dialogue made up of opportunities for mutual listening. Above all, it means that museums can assume the right degree of responsibility based on a model centered around visitors and their needs. On this subject, Lois H. Silverman highlights how this approach, and in particular the concept of meaning-making, "broadens our notion of the museum educator's role to be one who is knowledgeable in the ways people make meaning of objects and skilled in facilitating dialogue and negotiation."[4] Given that twenty years have passed since these considerations were first laid out, we can no longer justify the tendency to delegate this responsibility exclusively to those who deal with education. It is, however, interesting to note how these theories have more generally "revolutionized the field of professional practice," establishing the foundations of a new relationship between museum staff and visitors.[5]

This new concept of ideal parity between museum and visitor also raises questions of identity: By accepting that each object can take on multiple meanings and be as multifaceted as its audience, it becomes impossible to attach a single label to either. Dialogue and exploring meaning thus become central to a museum's process, founded on the knowledge that visitors are both deeply different from one another and extremely similar, as suggested by behavioral studies.

WHAT APPEARS PREDICTABLE

If, as we have seen, the museum space is complex by definition, the ways in which visitors interact with it are no less so. Every choice the museum makes has an impact on its audiences, affecting not only their active engagement with the meaning of what they are looking at, but their very behavior. Such considerations must obviously be made with an awareness of the irrationality that is inherent to each individual, but they also urge us to take into account the automatic cognitive behaviors that preface many interactions with both spaces and people.

Years of research confirm that "people see, read, remember"—as well as think, focus their attention, feel, make mistakes, and decide—in repetitive and often predictable ways, to paraphrase a well-known design psychology text. This classic, entitled *100 Things Every Designer Needs to Know about People*, is not the most academic of publications, but it has nonetheless become a valuable resource for anyone involved in design.[6] "People process information better in bite-sized chunks";[7] "people believe that things that are close together belong together";[8] and "unpredictability keeps people searching"[9] are concepts that have a lot to teach us, not only about people's thinking and behavior in general, but about those of visitors and access as well.

Unfortunately, museums have frequently underestimated these considerations in their environments, despite the fact that research in this field began back in the early twentieth century. Initially, these studies were based largely on empirical observation (as in Gilman's study on fatigue), but, as time went on, they acquired a more psychological and sociological dimension with greater scientific credibility. There is an ongoing need to update our work in light of the cultural, anthropological, and sociological changes underway (such as the impact of the digital on attention). Reflections from the world of design allow us to better understand current visitors while offering useful guidelines for the creation of effective learning environments. In other words, they provide us with a framework for staging "exhibitions that attract," based on an understanding of the "physical factors that support or limit the comfort and attention of visitors."[10] Even now, years after this research began, many findings remain valid, like the concept of museums as spaces in which objects compete for attention. For example, there are many in-built, automatic behaviors beyond our control (always subject to many factors), such as the tendency for Westerners to head toward the right, the fact that people cross a space more quickly when the exit is visible, or that the largest and most attention-grabbing objects become the cornerstones within an exhibition.[11] These aspects remain relevant in spite of the recipients, but certain studies are due for updates, especially in regard to the needs of people with sensory disabilities.

Our cognitive needs often precede all others, regardless of other, more specific needs. We know, for example, that a tactile exploration designed for blind or visually impaired people first requires a macroscopic understanding to be established before the attention can be focused on detail, an approach that is the basis of all human understanding. Consider just how invaluable a museum map or the index of a book can be. Here you have a perfect illustration of our need to understand the broader context before we can orient ourselves in terms of a particular piece of content.

These similarities in the museum experience do not, however, preclude the existence of many processes that diverge through a range of personal variables, such as the different relationships that expert and non-expert visitors have with the space. Alessandro Bollo and Luca Dal Pozzolo have observed that a visitor's level of cultural or specific knowledge is inversely proportional to the influence a space exerts.[12] In other words, a visitor who is less familiar with a museum feels a stronger obligation to follow the exhibition path laid out for them, while a frequent visitor feels more entitled to enjoy the space with greater freedom, a consideration that partially echoes Michael J. Parsons's conclusions regarding autonomy in interpretation.

Therefore, layers of conditioning and perceptions influence a museum experience, and the ways in which we approach a space lie beyond the realm of automatic behavior. A somewhat uncommon strategy for promoting change is that of spelling out aspects of the experience that are generally taken for granted. One example from Los Angeles shares possible modalities and tools favoring greater accessibility through a one-page brochure in which the Los Angeles County Museum of Art (LACMA) offered suggestions in English and Spanish for families who were likely to be less familiar with the museum.[13] It included tips like "Don't try to see everything: Twenty minutes to one hour is enough"; "Have a seat, you can sit on the floor"; and more. Such indications invited visitors into the space while promoting the learning of new behaviors that are not as obvious as they might seem.

HOW TO DEFINE VISITORS

Over the decades, we have witnessed a change not only in visitors, but also in the approaches used when trying to define them. This process has not always been linear, and the understanding of *who* visitors are has led to a progressively deeper investigation of the *why*. The reasons quickly become clear if we consider Eilean Hooper-Greenhill's declaration that it is no longer sufficient "to observe what people do" or even "to ask demographic questions." We must now seek out an analytical understanding by means of qualitative research.[14] Quantitative metrics, the same data that often guides the easiest segmentations in marketing, may prove insufficient for examining key aspects of design when used in isolation. What we need to understand is whether the homogeneity that governs our definition of certain groups brings about a distortion in our perception of them, amplifying certain information; in the case of people with disabilities, for example, we risk circumscribing their needs only to those related to their disability.

By asking new questions, we can explore new ways of looking at visitors. Pierre Bourdieu's work in this area, which highlights social injustices, is hands-down among the most influential examinations of the subject.[15] His art museum research relied on cross-examining various factors related to social class, occupation, age, education, income, and ethnicity in order to define both a theory and a critique of social inequality. His work remains highly relevant to this day.

In recent years, the debate around intersectionality has intensified and shed new light on the complexity of these issues. The term *intersectionality* was coined over thirty years ago by Kimberlé Crenshaw, a professor of law at Columbia University.[16] It outlines how individual characteristics that are subject to discrimination can overlap with one other, generating other forms of injustice: In the case of disability, people can suffer further when they are discriminated against not only because of their disability, but also because of gender, class, sexuality, or immigration status, to name a few. A person with a disability who is also African American, for example, may face prejudice and inequalities associated with their intersectional identity that amount differently than the sum of issues raised by disability and race.

The density of this interpretative framework allows us to examine ulterior barriers and implement new strategies to break them down. While this approach has proved essential in battling clusters based on discriminatory factors, it can sometimes hamper the development of new, inclusive clusters based on positive similarities. Such novel grouping is also necessary to empower individuals, not to mention the very discipline. This dynamic will reemerge later in the chapter.

Very different research has emerged from the interviews John Falk carried out with hundreds of visitors at the California Science Center in which he focused on personal motivations.[17] In particular, his study was geared toward understanding the reasons people visit museums, using a model that identifies five categories based on the purpose of their experience. Members of each category behave and learn differently and provide us with a predictive system that allows us to pinpoint broader needs based on specific identity-related motivations. Defined as *Explorers, Facilitators, Professionals/Hobbyists, Experience Seekers,* and *Rechargers*, these five groups should, therefore, be taken into account when planning activities and proposals if we want their respective needs to be met.

Falk's work on personal motivations has inspired a number of studies in recent years. For example, the Phoenix Art Museum developed a project of direct investigations entitled *I'm Here Gallery Guide Series*.[18] Winner of the 2015 EdCom Awards for Excellence, the series is aimed at the public and consists of a series of three guides that vary in color and content (*I'm here . . . with kids; I'm here . . . for the first time; I'm here . . . on a date*). Each guide, designed with an eye on the potential for social media sharing, was created to help visitors discover the collections. The reasons for their visits informed the museum guide's starting point. Though not geared explicitly toward accessibility, a resource like this creates an opportunity to segment people first on the basis of contingent factors and motivations, which suggests a huge potential for inclusivity.

Another noteworthy case on the front end of museum practice and visitor clustering was the result of a massive research effort that began in 2003 at the Dallas Museum of Art. The museum spent eight years studying people's preferences and behaviors, as well as how they connect to art, through a process that, once again, grew out of the desire to create an environment aligned with the characteristics and needs of visitors.[19] Beginning with an intensive survey, the museum was able to identify a series of clusters based on visitors' art viewing preferences.[20] In other words, the museum, in collaboration with an external organization involved in the research, sought out information that was useful for creating "memorable experiences with art, with lasting impact,"[21] without relying solely on traditional demographic information. This experience became well-known thanks to the publication of a book recounting its development, and has continued to evolve over the years.[22]

On its website, the Metropolitan Museum of Art also invites us to consider different perspectives: On the "Plan your visit" page, the options for booking a ticket are associated with four crosscutting needs: "I live in New York," "I am a student in NY, NJ, or CT," "I am visiting New York," or "I am a member."[23] Of course, each of these categories can also include, for example, people with disabilities (who will find specific pages on the website with answers to specific questions), but their needs to be considered seem more complex.

Although it has not always been correctly interpreted, Howard Gardner's work on intelligence types has also had a profound impact on the museum world.[24] According to the American psychologist and Harvard professor, there are seven kinds of intelligence: linguistic, logical-mathematical, musical, bodily-kinesthetic, spatial, interpersonal, and intrapersonal. Some people possess extremely high levels in all or most intelligence types, while others have developed a more pronounced intelligence in certain areas. An important takeaway from this work is the understanding that everyone has the ability to develop all of these intelligences to a satisfactory level. Over the years, this theory has received a tremendous amount of attention and success, especially in the field of education, although it has often been mistakenly associated with the concept of different learning styles, prompting the development of a diverse range of activities and engagement strategies. In spite of the mismatch between the original theory and the adopted practices, the outcome in museums has been significant and has led to the implementation of multimodal approaches that aim at improving access to these institutions.

Lastly, *spectrum personas* provide a completely different way of classifying people on the basis of their needs by examining purpose and context. According to the authors of the booklet *Inclusive: A Microsoft Design Toolkit*, exclusion is something we all experience every time we interact with a project whose mismatch of cognitive, sensory, and social needs is evident.[25] What the text lays out is not so much a theoretical framework as a real design tool. It defines personas based on sensory and cognitive mismatches (with regard to "touching," "talking," "seeing," and "hearing") across a spectrum of different time scenarios that may be permanent, temporary, or situational. Kat Holmes, one of the Microsoft designers involved in the project, considers video subtitles to be a useful example: fundamental for a deaf person (permanent scenario), for people in a busy airport (situational scenario), and even for those learning a new language (temporary scenario).[26] Clearly in this case it is mainly a matter of highlighting an already familiar concept in inclusive design, one that solves for one person and extends to many, but also of identifying new conformations and clusters with the potential to rehabilitate the perception of all.

Let's turn our focus back to visitors with disabilities. We can observe some of their undeniable, specific needs, but if we limit ourselves to viewing only those, we might fail to consider people's lifestyles, interests, and motivations, aspects that liken their visit to those of any other visitor. If we reverse conventional modalities and highlight visitors' similarities over their differences, we can start challenging some of the assumptions that prevent accessibility from achieving its deserved relevance.

VISITORS WITH DISABILITIES

Looking at people with disabilities through a new lens does not mean eliminating activities specifically aimed at removing certain barriers, nor leaving specific needs unaddressed; the point is to question whether this group is as homogeneous as often assumed. There are many complex elements involved in this discourse. For example, people who recognize and describe themselves in this group can find pleasure in spending time with other people with the same needs. From the museum's perspective, it is easier to plan activities for a uniform target, and available resources (budget, time, staff, training, etc.) do not always leave room for differentiated proposals. In addition, it is worth remembering how museum inclusivity varies from country to country. After years of neglect in many places, the needs of people with disabilities are only recently being considered and, for this reason, prioritized. Moreover, people with disabilities are those who face the most insurmountable barriers, making these the most urgent ones to dismantle. Perhaps more generally, we can argue that the proposals developed often depend more on cultural awareness of disability than on the level of disciplinary awareness in the museum context.

Whatever the frame of reference, when we talk about people with disabilities, we generally refer to individuals who can be characterized by having specific physical, sensory, or cognitive needs, or a combination thereof. So, museums are asked to guarantee equal participation through interventions in places that were largely inaccessible for decades by finding alternatives to existing designs or by adopting new solutions that follow a more universal scope. Due to the specific nature of certain needs, the world of design defines people with disabilities as "extreme users," or even "lead users," since they require the implementation of completely novel solutions. As such, we can regard them as drivers of innovation, a standpoint that rarely features in disability-oriented design in museums today.

Overall, this category of visitors remains under investigation. Museum environments rarely make services available for people with disabilities that cater to a user's most basic characteristics, like age or previous knowledge of the subject. This oversight means that accessibility will remain a paradox until we learn to address visitors' intrinsic and personal motivations. It is not enough to take compensatory action; we need to address people's interests and competence levels. The case of those with an invisible disability may choose not to make it explicit, posing different challenges still. For these museumgoers, we must ensure that accessing information at the entrance is as straightforward as possible while establishing high levels of accessibility for both autonomous and group visits. Additionally, it is vital that we recognize the value of adapting spaces, tools, materials, and educational proposals according to types of needs, and evaluate their suitability for mixed groups on a case-by-case basis.

Clearly, this does not imply that inclusive proposals (i.e., those in which people with and without disabilities participate together) should be compulsory. There are cases in which such initiatives are possible and others in which they are not, and the idea that this sort of "inclusion" should always be the goal is one of the most common misunderstandings in the field. There are, in fact, cases in which museums ensure greater well-being by offering homogeneously grouped visitors. It is always about freedom of choice. Many firsthand experiences testify that groups made up of people with the same disability have the advantage of allowing participants to relax more, knowing that everyone has similar resources available and needs to put in the same kind of effort. In addition, it would be counterproductive to push inclusive proposals on people with very different needs as, if not properly led, this could unwittingly generate further mismatches, uncomfortable situations, and distorted perceptions, especially in the case of severe cognitive disabilities.

More generally, biases often undermine the possibility of viewing people with disabilities as active patrons. Contrary to the way authorities sometimes impose regulations on individual organizations from "above," museums often have the autonomy to make financial decisions, yet this critical point often remains inadequately addressed. The possibility of not charging admission can be seen as justification for a lack of corresponding services. The perception of disability may also be distorted by the level of schooling evident in this category; in fact, these levels are lower than average and result from the many barriers present on an educational level. What these biases fail to consider is that disability is a fluid condition that knows no boundaries in terms of willingness to pay, culture, stage of life, social status, race, gender, sexuality, and more. In this sense, it should be noted that the development of DEI (Diversity, Equity, and Inclusion) strategies does not always include accessibility. This oversight was also confirmed in a recent publication by the Smithsonian Institute, which observed that the attempt to understand the barriers that limit access for minority and traditionally excluded groups sometimes fails to take this condition into account, despite the inevitable intersections between these groups.[27]

A MISSING AUDIENCE

All sectors of museum work are undergoing a democratization process that implies broadening audiences and cultivating audience diversity. To a great extent, the history of museums tells us that they have traditionally attracted somewhat uniform audiences, and today's data reveals this is still the case.[28] A museum's representativeness, however, is only relative to the extent to which they have succeeded in making themselves relevant to typically excluded audiences.

Thanks to a growing awareness in recent years, various countries have engaged in developing new projects that aim to reduce, or, more hopefully, eliminate, discrimination and barriers that limit the participation of many groups. These initiatives have included efforts to become more representative through the diversification of staff and improved communication strategies. Over the past decade, diversity has been one of the most significant themes to emerge in the museum world; there is a range of social phenomena gathering pace, pushing museums to decolonize (intended in the broadest sense of the term), and demanding change from the bottom up. It could therefore be argued that, despite everything, the museum sector possesses a driving force that is lacking in other cultural sectors.

We should, however, also look upstream at this phenomenon and note that museums are only part of a complex system that has always lived with the uncertain distinctions between integrated and marginal groups. In other words, the problem is not limited to barriers present in museums themselves, but it more often springs from socioeconomic issues that exist outside these institutions, like poor schooling, difficulty in accessing university education, the lack of subsidized social support, and the lack of museumgoing habits. Without absolving museums of all responsibility, it is worth remembering how many difficulties arise at earlier stages. For this reason, it is essential that we develop integrated approaches, including local initiatives with partner organizations.

An emblematic network can be found in Turin (Italy). It started from an impetus from St. Anna Hospital in 2009 when the institution sought to involve elements of civil society in promoting humanized paths of patient care. This approach aimed at making the hospital a place of learning and well-being in initiatives including art and culture. This project led to the development of a foundation and, moreover, to the creation of a large, interdisciplinary community that founded their work on an in-depth examination of international best practices.[29] Over the years, hundreds of empowering actions have been developed, and by 2014, one project emerged targeting museums: *Nati con la Cultura* (Born with Culture) was launched that same year.[30] It initially involved two entities, the St. Anna Hospital and a single museum, but the project is now being disseminated across a number of Italian hospitals as well as municipalities. On the one hand, this project aims at sensitizing museums toward child-friendly proposals and helps them define their initiatives' design. On the other hand, it offers each new family that gives birth a "cultural passport" that allows free admission to local museums up through the child's first birthday. This proposal was developed in conjunction with a heated debate around issues of *ius soli* (birthright citizenship), which, to date, is not foreseen in Italy, meaning that citizenship is not acquired as a result of the legal fact of being born in the country.

In and around Turin, the region of Piedmont alone now boasts forty child-friendly museums. These institutions have developed new skills relating to accessibility, offering spaces of mutual assistance and encounter, enabling effective connections with families in moments of particular need. More recently, this articulated path is investigating how to break the chains of inequality. One particular proposal addresses educational poverty by training medical personnel and obstetricians, while involving early childhood schools together with museums in using tools like literacy and music to empower a greater number of children and families.

Museums and their functions are undoubtedly changing. What was considered a merely educational role a few years ago has now taken on true political value, implying a range of action that includes structured social activism and listening. It remains fundamental, however, for this approach to be free of philanthropic and humanitarian leanings (which in the past seemed implicit in the concept of community) that all too often accompany these conversations. As Bernadette Lynch, honorary researcher at University College London, recalls, "The main aspect of this failure was the disabling effect of treating people as beneficiaries instead of active agents, thus continuing a notion of center-periphery social improvement that permeated what was offered as democratic practice."[31] On this subject, it is worth noting that while this area of study has habitually focused on the removal of systemic barriers that prevent certain social groups from accessing museums, the discipline has hesitated to accept the idea that, for some, museums may simply not be interesting places.

In the conversation around accessibility, we often forget about non-visitors, that is, those who do not visit museums for various reasons other than the presence of barriers. We are well aware of the motivations for the choices of those who decide to enter, but we are less informed about those who choose not to. People who deal with social issues in museums have promoted the message that museums are meaningful places, which is sometimes true; however, this insistence has inadvertently resulted in the creation of yet another "outgroup" and fails to fathom that not all museums are as generative as hoped.

Heritage can certainly have civic relevance, but if the subject remains the museum, we need to take a good look at each institution's ability to mediate between values and people. Otherwise, we amplify a rhetoric that remains difficult to undermine by assigning a value judgment that distinguishes between museumgoers and non-museumgoers. Although this area remains underexplored, we must seek to dispel the assumption that a person who does not enjoy museums automatically comes from a culturally deprived and marginalized background. This subtlety is overlooked and often leads to confusion in the battle for accessibility.

We must start by removing all possible barriers as a response to essential democratic principles. Upon achieving this, however, we must have no scruples about a person's right not to be interested in what museums have to offer. This means ensuring that people are listened to and treated with the respect they deserve. Furthermore, it would behoove us to be mindful of judgments that may prove ill-founded. In the coming years, it will be interesting to follow the momentum around these issues and see whether the profound digital transformations we witnessed during the COVID-19 pandemic will pave the way for new developments.

NOTES

1. Seph Rodney, *Personalization of the Museum Visit: Art Museums, Discourse, and Visitors* (London: Routledge, 2018), loc. 645 of 4060, Kindle.
2. George E. Hein, "Is Meaning Making Constructivism? Is Constructivism Meaning Making?" *Exhibitionist* 18, no. 2 (1999); Lois H. Silverman, "Meaning Making Matters: Communication, Consequences, and Exhibit Design," *Exhibitionist* 18, no. 2 (1999).
3. Eilean Hooper-Greenhill, *Museum, Media, Message* (London: Routledge, 1999), 7.
4. Lois H. Silverman, "Making Meaning Together: Lessons from the Field of American History," in *Transforming Practice: Selections from the Journal of Museum Education, 1992–1999*, ed. Joanne S Hirsch and Lois H. Silverman (London: Routledge, 2006), 233.
5. Rodney, *Personalization*, pos. 698 of 4060, Kindle.
6. Susan Weinschenk, *100 Things Every Designer Needs to Know about People* (San Francisco: New Riders, 2020).
7. Ibid., 62.
8. Ibid., 21.
9. Ibid., 123.
10. George Hein, *Learning in the Museum* (Abingdon, OX: Routledge, 1998), 136.
11. Stephen Bitgood, *Social Design in Museums: The Psychology of Visitor Studies*, 2 vols. (Edinburgh: MuseumsEtc, 2011).
12. Alessandro Bollo and Luca dal Pozzolo, "Analysis of Visitor Behaviour inside the Museum: An Empirical Study," Proceedings of the *8th International Conference on Arts and Cultural Management*, 2005, International Association of Arts and Cultural Management, Montreal, Canada, Article 28, http://neumann.hec.ca/aimac2005/PDF_Text/BolloA_DalPozzoloL.pdf.
13. The brochure was retrieved by the author during a visit to the museum in August 2014.
14. Eilean Hooper-Greenhill, "Studying Visitors," in *A Companion to Museum Studies*, ed. Susan McDonald (Malden, MA: Blackwell Publishing Ltd, 2006), 373.
15. Pierre Bourdieu, *Distinction: A Social Critique of the Judgement of Taste* (Cambridge, MA: Harvard University Press, 1989).

16. Kimberlé Crenshaw, "Demarginalizing the Intersection of Race and Sex: A Black Feminist Critique of Antidiscrimination Doctrine, Feminist Theory and Antiracist Politics," *University of Chicago Legal Forum* 1, no. 8 (1989), 139–67.
17. John Falk, *Identity and the Museum Visitor Experience* (Walnut Creek, CA: Left Coast Press, Inc., 2009).
18. "Design Sprints for Content Development: How Phoenix Art Museum Ran a Design Sprint," *Design Thinking for Museums*, accessed April 2, 2021, https://designthink ingformuseums.net/2016/05/17/design-sprints-for-content-development/; American Alliance of Museums, "EdCom Newsletter," February 2016, www.aam-us.org/wp-content/uploads/2018/09/february-2016-newsletter.pdf.
19. Bonnie Pitman and Ellen Cochran Hirzy, *Ignite the Power of Art: Advancing Visitor Engagement in Museums* (New Haven, CT: Yale University Press, 2011).
20. Ibid.
21. Ibid., 21.
22. Ibid.
23. The Metropolitan Museum of Art, "Plan your visit," accessed April 7, 2021, https://www.metmuseum.org/visit/plan-your-visit.
24. Howard Gardner, *Frames of Mind: The Theory of Multiple Intelligences* (New York: Basic Books, 1983).
25. "Microsoft Inclusive Design Booklet," Microsoft, accessed April 11, 2021, https://www.microsoft.com/design/inclusive/.
26. Kat Holmes, *Mismatch: How Inclusion Shapes Design* (Cambridge: The MIT Press, 2020), 104.
27. Beth Ziebarth, Janice Majewski, Robin Marquis, and Nancy Proctor, eds., *Inclusive Digital Interactives: Best Practices + Research* (Washington, DC: Access Smithsonian, Institute for Human Centered Design and MuseWeb, 2020), https://access.si.edu/sites/default/files/inclusive-digital-interactives-best-practices-research.pdf.public/file+downloads/Inclusive+Digital+Interactives+Best+Practices+%2B+Research .pdf.
28. For more recent visitor data, check: Betty Farrell et al., *Demographic Transformation and the Future of Museums* (Washington, DC: AAM Press American Association of Museums, 2010), www.aam-us.org/wp-content/uploads/2017/12/Demographic-Change-and-the-Future-of-Museums.pdf; Colleen Dilenschneider, "Active Visitors: Who Currently Attends Cultural Organizations?," *Colleen Dilenschneider: Know Your Own Bone*, January 23, 2019, accessed June 20, 2021, www.colleendilen .com/2019/01/23/active-visitors-currently-attends-cultural-organizations-data/.
29. Fondazione Medicina a Misura di Donna, accessed July 21, 2021, https://www .medicinamisuradidonna.it/.
30. Nati con la Cultura, accessed July 21, 2021, http://www.naticonlacultura.it/.
31. Bernadette Lynch, *Whose Cake Is It Anyway? A Collaborative Investigation into Engagement and Participation in Twelve Museums and Galleries in the UK* (London: Paul Hamlyn Foundation, 2011), www.phf.org.uk/publications/whose-cake-anyway.

4

Current Challenges

ONLINE ACCESSIBILITY AND THE PANDEMIC

Discussing museum accessibility deals with more than physical contexts; it in-cludes a multitiered process made up of many steps and strategies, of which digital contributions form part and parcel. Hence this chapter, unlike the others, will not focus on a strategic dimension but will delve into specific issues regarding digital projects and solutions, as well as the opportunities and challenges they pose today. When developed proactively, tools and resources like websites, social media, and apps improve access to cultural content. Moreover, digital services actually help shape a single, consolidated visitor experience when combined with the physical experience, and they can confer credibility—or not—to a museum's commitment to inclusiveness.

In 2020, the spread of the pandemic undeniably accelerated development in this field, providing plenty of inspiration for reflection on accessibility. To limit the diffusion of the COVID-19 virus, many museums around the world were forced to close and were compelled to devise new strategies to keep in touch with their au-diences. For most, digital and online activities proved the best way to go, promoting a wide range of initiatives with very different results, especially in terms of access. Although the solutions developed in the early stages were dictated by urgency (and, therefore, often largely inattentive to user needs), the following months allowed many organizations to develop more sophisticated tools and ideas. It became clear, however, that the skills and good practices employed in digital accessibility were more limited than those widely implemented within museums themselves, requiring specific expertise and with fewer models for reference. For this reason, the outcomes of these experiences diverge greatly, due also to the varying resources museums had at their disposal, as well as the degree of attention paid to digital accessibility in all its forms.

Digital technology has presented us with a paradoxical contradiction: On the one hand, it constitutes a vital tool for expanding the spectrum of potential recipients; on the other, it limits access whenever it lacks a clear inclusion strategy. It is evident that digital media have not reached as many people as originally thought. In fact, the most vulnerable remain the most disadvantaged, namely "people with low literacy or not fluent in the language, people with low bandwidth connections or using older technologies, new and infrequent users, and mobile device users," as well as people with disabilities.[1] With this in mind, it is not hard to understand why a few museums have chosen to launch digital programs together with analog alternatives like dance lessons or guided tours offered by phone. However, a survey conducted by the Network of European Museum Organisations (NEMO) found that more than 60 percent of museums in Europe have built up their online presence, with 30 percent asking staff to cover new tasks.[2] Museums have enhanced existing content and created new offerings, but the quality remains to be determined.

For example, the Museum, Arts and Culture Access Consortium (MAC) reported substantial changes and an increasing awareness of certain needs over the course of New York's lockdowns. This organization aims to increase access to NYC's cultural institutions for the disability community "through connection, education, and advocacy."[3] The context in which this reality takes shape has an excellent track record in accessibility: New York City has historically stood out as a virtuous exception on the global level. The city's museums and cultural organizations often serve as transformative models for institutions in other states and countries.

Given these premises, the findings of a recent MAC study of online content, dissemination, and accessibility are extremely interesting. Throughout 2020, the consortium launched Mapping Virtual Access in Cultural Institutions (MVACI), a research project that sought to understand the changes in digital access that occurred in the months of the pandemic in cultural organizations.[4] Hence they conducted a series of interviews, a survey, and online workshops. They listened to dozens of local organizations, whose experience and knowledge was then shared in a number of online appointments that involved many realities. These meetings, open to all, have allowed us to focus on new needs and new barriers, but above all to identify new digital opportunities to encourage participation, especially that of people with disabilities.

Many relevant considerations emerged from the initial mapping, shared in the first Zoom meeting; they can be summarized as follows.[5] First, most of the fifty-five institutions surveyed reformulated their programs through live online events, recorded and posted lectures, and webinars (95 percent); others hosted performances (80 percent), and increased their use of social media (67 percent). Just over 20 percent of respondents used tools like email or the phone. Steps were taken to make online content more accessible: 74 percent worked on image description (alt-text, audio, auto-description), 62 percent used automatic captions, and 53 percent preferred live captions, like CART. More than half created contexts with "relaxed" participation (especially with regard to live events) by making suggestions like turning off the cameras to participants or offering modes of interaction only via chat. Others offered interpretation with sign language (45 percent), wrote "a document listing best practices for virtual access" (40 percent), or created specific content for adults and children with intellectual disabilities (32 percent). The least-adopted strategies were website access audits, the use of plain language, and the definition of virtual verbal description tours; fewer still involved external consultants. Amidst the vast amount of collected information, it is also important to mention the barriers that prevented the implementation of accessible programs. In descending order of implementation, these included: budget restrictions, lack of institutional knowledge, furloughs/layoffs, facilitating online lessons, lack of external engagement, and burnout. Barriers to the development of accessibility itself are also often found on-site.

These cultural institutions suggested next steps to take to make their program more accessible through virtual content, and they offered ideas for promoting accessibility through organizational management. These were:

1. Including more people with disabilities in leadership;
2. Offering more training to cultural institution staff;
3. Sharing more online content created by people with disabilities; and
4. Partnering with organizations such as MAC, NYC DCLA (Department of Cultural Affairs), or CCAC (Chicago Cultural Accessibility Consortium).

The MVACI project, funded by the FAR Fund, has currently obtained funding renewal that will allow for the study's implementation.

Data emerging from this research clearly provide a glimpse of the sector's potential that requires precise interventions. Many of the proposals that have emerged in the digital world will become fixtures in expanding museum accessibility. It is impossible to predict the degree to which remote fruition will be imposed, but we can no longer dismiss the advantages of blended offerings.

The digital realm has become more relevant than ever, and recent historical events compel us to regard it as an essential ally. The following pages will highlight some basic aspects that mainly characterize web accessibility for people with disabilities and indications for hosting successful virtual tours with a focus on cognitive issues. These resources have demonstrated their value in long-distance relationships, but they need further attention as to how to adapt their content to audiences' different needs as they inevitably undergo significant developments.

FROM ONLINE TO ON-SITE ACCESSIBILITY

Over the years, online functions, especially those featured on websites, have become so sophisticated that they are no longer adjunct additions to physical components. This aspect promises to enrich the museum experience through online services, games, shops, opportunities to learn more about collections, and more.[6]

While accessibility is perhaps better known in the digital realm, digital access has not always seen equal attention in the field of museums where its efforts have been fairly circumscribed, even when developing tools such as apps, platforms, or social media. Making each of these instruments accessible requires different approaches and expertise that, in the case of a museum website, can be summarized in the following and far-from-exhaustive list:

- Offering detailed information about the accessible facilities available in the physical space;
- Allowing access to dialogues, content, text, and images that can provide equally satisfying experiences, regardless of visitors' different needs;
- Foreseeing the option of downloading preparatory materials and support tools for the visit, like social stories, maps, etc.;
- Providing alternative formats to access contents during the visit, like audio, text, or images; and
- Facilitating engagement and bolstering motivation to the visit.

The following pages will focus mainly on a few items listed above to highlight the ease with which we can adopt certain solutions while keeping in mind the technical complexity of others.

In planning accessible websites, it is of primary importance to consider how these spaces fulfill the express purpose of providing useful information for a visit, particularly for those who need to have specific answers before going to the museum. Acquiring detailed knowledge of the facilities available on-site is essential, especially given that services like educational activities or guided tours are often provided only within limited timeslots. After all, communicating accessibility is itself an integral component of the discipline. We can only help people know what we offer if we have adequate communication strategies in place and if we clearly define the most suitable channels for conveying that information. The following examples can help illustrate this point.

Online, our first concern is undoubtedly to position the page dedicated to accessibility while clearly explaining the steps needed to get there from the home page. In English-speaking countries, this page is typically found under the heading "Visit," but there are numerous alternatives. If people know where to find a page, by extension, it becomes more accessible. For the same reason, having an internal search box can still be useful. Another key concern is the comprehensibility of text and information. It is always best to use plain language and to present text in the most legible form by using easy-to-read fonts, short sentences, correct spacing, and frequent paragraph breaks. This attention to understandability must, however, be applied consistently. In terms of content, the accessibility page should provide as much information as possible, including a list of available amenities and tools, as well as details about any potential barriers, such as those of a temporary nature (like a broken stair lift).

Chapter 4

Detailed descriptions are always better, but they need to be presented synthetically and possibly through a rational list. For example, in its page on accessibility, the British Museum states, "The main entrance on Great Russell Street has 12 steps with a handrail," a useful piece of information for people who struggle with mobility or have visual impairments.[7] Other relevant information includes the "Quieter times" and "Quieter areas" of the museum and describes these in some detail. Many large museums choose to highlight this aspect with the aid of sensory-friendly maps, as we will see further on.

Pages dedicated to access sometimes tend to offer a wealth of information but differ in the criteria they apply. The Canadian Museum of Human Rights, well known for its impressive work in inclusive design, distinguishes between three aspects of the visit and explains the existing facilities around the museum, the mobile app, and in the galleries.[8]

Constant updates are essential to the effectiveness of the accessibility page. The Metropolitan Museum of Art, for instance, makes explicit the impact of "Covid-19 Safety Measures on Visitors with Disabilities" in view of the fact that certain services are currently unavailable for health and safety reasons.[9] Essential information that should be included on the accessibility page can be summarized as follows:

- Information about the entrance and ticketing;
- A short description of existing facilities like Assistive Listening Systems, Sighted Guide Tours, ASL Interpreters/CART reporting, mobility, large print guide, family sensory support backpacks, etc.;
- COVID-19 safety measures and how they might affect the experience of visitors with disabilities;
- Information available in an accessible format;
- Restrooms, including their locations and accessibility;
- Service animal policies;
- Transport/parking information;
- Gallery seating information;
- Lighting and temperature;
- A downloadable map (including a sensory map);
- Information about quieter visit times and areas (especially for large museums);
- Food/bar and restaurant facilities (including options for dietary restrictions);
- Online accessibility, including activities and proposals;
- Contact information for access coordinators or staff involved in accessibility (both by phone and email).

Finally, these webpages are increasingly likely to feature an accessibility statement that conveys the institution's commitment to access, shares aims, and lays out the accessibility standards in use. In addition to a detailed description of available accommodations, some museums also provide the accessibility coordinator's contact information in the form of both a phone number and an email address.

We should note that detailing such information on the accessibility page requires minimal effort, an effort that is repaid in full through its undeniable value to the audience. Matthew Cock of Vocal Eyes, a UK charity engaged in outreach work, offers further suggestions to boost the effectiveness of this webpage.[10] He suggests: "Use a range of media (images, video and audio) as well as descriptive text" and "Inform visitors if front-of-house staff have had awareness or other relevant training, and how to identify them." As always, it is important to follow up with museumgoers to be sure that the information provided is useful and thorough.

BEING FOR ALL

It is vital to use simple language, offer a range of formats, and facilitate usability while providing necessary information for a visit, but these approaches might not suffice. To become a truly valuable resource, websites must offer an experience that is equitable and fully accessible to all. For this to happen, a series of essential measures and methods must be adopted, especially for those who use assistive technologies like hardware and software (such as voice dictation, screen magnifiers, screen readers, and so on), which enable independent access through the employment of some basic requirements. For example, if images are missing a description or the content is organized with a faulty hierarchy, there is the risk that digital access through screen readers (programs that read text onscreen through voice synthesis or a braille bar) or other assistive technology may be invalidated. We can make a number of mistakes without realizing it; they range from incorrect color contrast to videos without subtitles, a lack of search functions, nondescriptive links, and the list goes on.

To help improve website accessibility, the Web Accessibility Initiative (WAI) of the World Wide Web Consortium (W3C) developed an exhaustive framework for all adoptable solutions and has thus created what is commonly recognized as the main international guidelines.[11] Within these guidelines, for example, images must be described using a form of written text known as "Alt text," which stands for "alternative text." This means that those who are unable to see the images can use a screen reader to listen to a description of them. Alt text favors short, clear, and understandable descriptions and must be assigned to every image that contains relevant content, to be defined together with titles and captions.

Recently, the Cooper Hewitt Museum was able to draw up extremely detailed guidelines for short- and long-image descriptions with numerous accompanying examples, thanks to a thorough joint-designed project carried out in-house, using their own digital collections.[12] Adhering to these guidelines reveals how these complex issues require ethical guidelines and thoughtful interpretation. For instance, descriptions inevitably raise questions about identity, gender, and race that are at the forefront of modern debate, themes taken into close consideration by this project.

The Museum of Contemporary Art in Chicago has also been working on these themes. In an effort to translate more than eighteen thousand images archived on its website, the museum, together with Sina Bahram's team, has developed an open-source toolkit, available online, to create and publish visual descriptions.[13] This innovative software, called Coyote, was designed "to support workflow around the description of images"[14] on the museum's revamped website, but it has also become a valuable tool for finding works of art in the database and online. The descriptions were composed by volunteers from a variety of areas, including curators, educators, librarians, publishing and digital team members, and staff from visitor services, exhibitions, and collections,[15] and, as at Cooper Hewitt, the process seems to have created opportunities for raising awareness about making museum content accessible to visitors who use screen readers[16] for museum staff across the board.

These two examples show how just describing images is becoming as fundamental as defining a hierarchy of content, whatever that content may be. Text and images must be positioned according to a logic that extends beyond the obvious, with content categorized and assigned to different levels. This kind of structure allows assistive technology to approach website information sequentially, starting with general titles, then proceeding to subtitles, then paragraphs, and lastly text. Naturally, this must all be done without affecting the graphic experience of those who explore the site visually.

Audio description and captioning is key for making video content accessible to people with sensory disabilities, via websites, apps, social media, and virtual meetings. Audio description involves the creation of additional audio tracks in which a voice recounts a video including significant aspects that may not be verbally explicit. This practice gives access to elements that viewers generally grasp through images, like details of the setting, a description of important action, or the introduction of a character as they appear on screen. Captioning follows the same principle, but relays dialogue and non-speech audio as written text. Captions differ from subtitles in that they provide contextual information in addition to text. These may be defined as *closed* or *unclosed* according to whether or not they are included directly in the video. Alongside captions, for deaf audiences, it is also important to provide transcripts that can be read independently of the video itself. Another suggested solution is the use of video recording in which an interpreter uses sign language to make the experience as understandable as possible.

Following well-researched guidelines minimizes the risk of mistakes. In addition to the ones already cited, we would recommend those outlined by the Carnegie Museums of Pittsburgh, available online.[17] For a more complete look at the entire subject with an in-depth focus on best practices and cases, it is worth reading *Inclusive Digital Interactives: Best Practices + Research*, a publication recently released by the Smithsonian.[18]

VISIT SUPPORT TOOLS

Websites also serve the essential purpose of sharing content before or during a visit. The simple option for visitors to download support materials is an increasingly widespread practice that generates an array of access opportunities. Tools like maps (including sensory ones), social stories, and inclusion cards (together with video transcripts, audio descriptions, or other resources) constitute additional content that may prove useful for visitors, particularly those with neurodivergent disorders and their caregivers.

Maps are a particularly effective tool when it comes to cognitive and sensory accessibility. Since COVID restricted museums from distributing them in the museum itself, the pandemic has increased the need to include them among online resources. For institutions with complex layouts, it is necessary to provide a simple, yet faithful depiction of public spaces through contrasting color and audio cues, alongside more traditional strategies for improving legibility. The last few years have seen the gradual spread of sensory maps, which can often be downloaded from the website and allow visitors to identify sensory-friendly spaces in the museum. Designed especially for visitors on the autism spectrum, these maps are intended to support anyone who is sensitive to factors like crowds, light, and noise, indicating the quietest areas or alerting them to the busier ones. Some examples can easily be found online, such as the one provided by the Museum of London, or even via an app, as for the maps made for the Chicago's Children's Museum, the Shedd Aquarium, and the Field Museum.[19]

Social stories offer another important resource often aimed at first-time visitors, families, or visitors with developmental disabilities. This narrative form, which originated not in museum practice but in an educational context, usually takes the form of a short, written story that revolves around social skills, situations, concepts, and rules of behavior, introducing the visit step by step. More recently, these stories have been told not just in text, but also through video. In museum practice, social stories are simple but effective tools that allow people to familiarize themselves in advance with the situations they will encounter during their visit experience. They might come in the form of a booklet or visual checklist, with photos and easy-to-read texts that offer a linear outline of modes of access to the museum, how to get to the reception area, and the rules to follow throughout the visit. For example, those developed by the American Museum of Natural History have been recently updated and include suggestions regarding the use of masks and temperature control.[20]

For visitors on the autism spectrum in particular, the Metropolitan Museum website offers one of the largest collections of resources. In addition to those already mentioned above, its many tools and programs include My Met Tour, a visual checklist with picture cards developed to help parents and children design their own visit.[21]

Alongside these forms of support, for instance, we can also provide digital captions for objects (if they are not already present in an app), which allow visitors to benefit from adaptable content that can be enlarged or listened to as needed. Overall, it is important to keep in mind a solution's usability as well as the quality of the experience as a whole.

In parallel, museums can promote professional development in a number of fields by creating accessible online resources to be used in training and refresher courses aimed at coworkers. One such museum is the Museum of Modern Art (MoMA), whose website features a series of accessible videos created as a training tool for museum professionals working both in education and accessibility. Some of these resources stem from the MoMA Alzheimer's Project, launched in 2006 with the goal of making the museum accessible to people with Alzheimer's disease or other forms of dementia and their family members or care partners. The resulting website now contains a wealth of content, research tools, and practical examples useful in supporting the international dissemination of accessibility practices designed by the museum itself.[22]

COGNITIVE CONSTRAINTS: THE CASE FOR VIRTUAL TOURS

In their book *Universal Principles of Design*, William Lidwell, Kritina Holden, and Jill Butler address the concept of good design and the importance of establishing a "hierarchy of needs": We must be sure to respond first and foremost to basic necessities in order to achieve set goals.[23] Based on Maslow's theory of human needs, they envision a pyramid that starts with the fulfillment of people's fundamental requirements before addressing more sophisticated ones on higher levels. Digital offerings should be designed similarly, starting on the most basic level with functionality and accessibility, then building up to reliability, usability, proficiency, and creativity respectively. Naturally, we often find that digital contexts remain shaky at the base of the pyramid, much like offline spaces.

This contrast often emerges in so-called virtual tours, which were limited to virtual experiences simulating actual experience. These gained a lot of attention, especially in 2020, when museums around the world were forced to close their doors. These proposals provide useful prompts to reflect on the meaning of not only sensory, but especially cognitive accessibility. They reveal a series of barriers that are just as subtle as they are significant. In fact, even a cursory analysis of the limitations on a cognitive level suggests that we need to rethink not only the hierarchy of their design needs, but even their own purpose.

Virtual tours can take many forms, including live or prerecorded guided tours led by people or even robots, but they usually pay little attention to visitors' basic needs. For instance, they often fail to share their basic goals with visitors or provide them with orientation tools. Sometimes they lack differentiated stimuli and interpretive articulation even though these are essential for rendering an experience accessible. Such shortcomings compound the issue of sensory barriers, made even more evident when alt-text, captions, transcripts, and audio description are missing. When offering prerecorded tours, these resources can be furnished more easily.

Virtual tours typically explore museum spaces, whether real or digitally re-created, through which the visitor can move either independently or accompanied by a guide. Even in an online scenario, the greatest challenge remains that of sustaining a visitor's attention. In fact, as opposed to an on-site tour, an unsatisfactory virtual experience can be cut off almost instantly thanks to the ease with which we can leave a website. This difficulty is compounded by the absence of intermediary figures, as well as the constant distractions we are subject to when sitting at a computer.

This first level of complexity is often exacerbated by other challenging issues, which appear to be at least partly unresolved. Virtual tours, for instance, frequently neglect to communicate or even clearly establish their objectives. This unconscious shortcoming is often counterproductive since it generates cognitive dissonance. There are many examples to choose from, but one of the most striking is the frequent inability to bring a piece of artwork into sharp focus, especially in real settings. While art and object content often suffer in virtual tours, audiences can gain only a clearer idea of the museum's layout and architecture, which is usually not the main aim of a visit. Google Art has made a great commitment in this area and has achieved extraordinary results. For example, the platform presents more than just objects by suggesting different observation strategies and focusing progressively on different details. One example is Vermeer's painting *The Milkmaid*, which can be viewed and heard on the Rijksmuseum website, thanks to the inclusion of both an image and audio descriptions.[24] The aim of this project is to equip the visitor with skills that prove useful when visiting the museum in person. The objective is clear and moves away from the more traditional approach, limited to contemplation, a habit that is effective and accessible to a much smaller array of visitors.

Another aspect that severely hampers cognitive accessibility is the lack of orientation. Offerings of this kind generally open the visitor experience toward a predetermined starting point without sharing the overall framework or destination. While a physical trip to the museum will allow visitors to get a rough idea of the space's size and layout (usually thanks to a map), the virtual experience is often missing these references altogether. Sometimes a map of the museum is not even made available online, giving the audience the sense of making their way through a labyrinth. This awareness should not be confused with the Principle of Progressive Disclosure, the choice to provide only relevant information at a given time so as not to overload the recipient.

As heritage interpretation expert John Veverka reminds us, a tour cannot simply be a route from A to B, but it should lead the visitor through a process of discovery, helping them explore a range of overlapping sensations and stimuli offered by the museum.[25] If we are unable to provide different strategies for interaction and learning, the current experience of a virtual tour feels more like losing yourself within a flat surface, much like the surface of a computer screen.

These issues come to the fore in the use of Beam, a famous tele-robot used as an accessibility tool that allows those who are unable to get to the museum to embark on telepresence tours. A few institutions have recently made this robot available for paid guided tours. It can be controlled remotely by the user, but direct experience reveals that it is difficult to observe objects or move fluidly throughout the museum space. In fact, Beam does not respond well to commands, moves very slowly, and may be equipped with a poor-quality camera; these elements make a visit possible for many, but the experience lacks usability and often remains confusing and unsatisfactory.

While tele-robots and other technologies will evolve over time, it is essential to remember that accessibility amounts to more. This field aims to give visitors accessible content in a simple, fulfilling, and thoughtful manner. With this awareness in mind, the hope today is that digital technology can help us understand and live significant and complex experiences, facilitating access to anyone who is interested and in need, while increasing consciousness of these issues.

By implementing these tools, many museums have the opportunity to improve sensitivity and raise interest in the field, also by involving colleagues from other sectors. With museums reopening and returning to full operations, the hope is that institutions will manage to hold on to what they have learned and continue to roll out more effective programs and initiatives. This goal can only be reached if shared by all disciplines of museum practice and implemented throughout careful planning strategy and design process.

NOTES

1. "Web Accessibility Initiative (WAI)," World Wide Web Consortium, accessed April 8, 2021, https://www.w3.org/WAI/.
2. Network of European Museum Organisations (NEMO), "Survey on the impact of the COVID-19 situation on museums in Europe Final Report," May 12, 2020, accessed April 7, 2021, https://www.ne-mo.org/fileadmin/Dateien/public/NEMO_documents/NEMO_COVID19_Report_12.05.2020.pdf.
3. "About us," Museum, Arts and Culture Access Consortium (MAC), accessed June 21, 2021, https://macaccess.org/about-new/.
4. "Meet Our Grants: Mapping Virtual Access in Cultural Institutions," Museum, Arts and Culture Access Consortium (MAC), accessed June 21, 2021, https://macaccess.org/meet-our-grants-mapping-virtual-access-in-cultural-institutions/.
5. *Mapping Virtual Access Together* was a series of events organized within the project Mapping Virtual Access in Cultural Institutions Committee (MVACI), coordinated by project manager Bojana Coklyat and informed by research done throughout the pandemic. The meetings, aimed at sharing findings with the participants, took place in 2021 and included different speakers and cultural institutions.
6. Maria Elena Colombo, *Musei e cultura digitale. Fra narrativa, pratiche e testimonianze* (Torino: Editrice Bibliografica, 2020).
7. "Accessibility at the Museum," the British Museum, accessed April 3, 2021, http://www.britishmuseum.org/visit/accessibility-museum.
8. "Accessibility," Canadian Museum of Human Rights, accessed February 23, 2021, https://humanrights.ca/visit/accessibility.
9. "Accessibility," the Metropolitan Museum of Art, accessed February 23, 2021, www.metmuseum.org/visit/accessibility.

10. Matthew Cock, "Web Accessibility. Making Websites Accessible to All Is an Important Responsibility," *Museum Association Journal*, November 16, 2018, accessed April 12, 2021, https://www.museumsassociation.org/museums-journal/in-practice/2018/11/16112018-web-accessibility-mp/.

11. WAI, World Wide Web Consortium.

12. "Cooper Hewitt Guidelines for Image Description," Cooper Hewitt, Smithsonian Design Museum, 2019, accessed April 11, 2021, www.cooperhewitt.org/cooper-hewitt-guidelines-for-image-description/; Ruth Starr, "Prioritizing Image Descriptions and Digital Equity at Cooper Hewitt," *American Alliance of Museums*, May 13, 2020, accessed March 20, 2021, https://www.aam-us.org/2020/05/13/prioritizing-image-descriptions-and-digital-equity-at-cooper-hewitt/.

13. Sina Bahram, Susan Chun, and Anna Chiaretta Lavatelli, "Using Coyote to Describe the World," *MW18: Museums and the Web 2018*, April 17, 2018, accessed April 15, 2021, https://mw18.mwconf.org/paper/using-coyote-to-describe-the-world/.

14. "Case Study: MCA Chicago," Coyote, accessed April 12, 2021, https://coyote.pics/resources/case-study-mca-chicago/.

15. Ibid.

16. Ibid.

17. "Overview | Accessibility Guidelines," Carnegie Museums, accessed April 15, 2021, http://web-accessibility.carnegiemuseums.org/.

18. Beth Ziebarth, Janice Majewski, Robin Marquis, and Nancy Proctor, eds., *Inclusive Digital Interactives: Best Practices + Research* (Washington, DC: Access Smithsonian, Institute for Human Centered Design and MuseWeb, 2020), https://access.si.edu/sites/default/files/inclusive-digital-interactives-best-practices-research.pdf.public/file+downloads/Inclusive+Digital+Interactives+Best+Practices+%2B+Research.pdf.

19. "Museum Accessibility," Museum of London, accessed May 23, 2021, https://www.museumoflondon.org.uk/museum-london/plan-your-visit/museum-accessibility; Jenee Iyer, "New Apps Focus on Autism Inclusivity," Arts Management and Technology Laboratory, March 17, 2017, accessed May 4, 2021, https://amt-lab.org/reviews/2017/2/new-apps-focus-on-autism-inclusivity.

20. "Social Story for the American Museum of Natural History," American Museum of Natural History, accessed July 18, 2021, https://www.amnh.org/content/download/323244/4997726/file/Social%20Story%20AMNH.pdf.

21. "My Met Tour," the Metropolitan Museum of Art, accessed May 16, 2021, https://www.metmuseum.org/-/media/files/events/programs/progs-for-visitors-with-disabilities/my-met-tour.pdf.

22. "Museum Training Resources | MoMA," the Museum of Modern Art, accessed April 7, 2021, https://www.moma.org/visit/accessibility/resources.

23. William Lidwell, Kritina Holden, and Jill Butler, *Universal Principles of Design: 125 Ways to Enhance Usability, Influence Perception, Increase Appeal, Make Better Design Decisions, and Teach through Design*, 2nd ed. (Beverly, MA: Rockport Publishers, 2010).

24. "Rijksmuseum," Google Arts & Culture, accessed April 7, 2021, https://artsandculture.google.com/partner/rijksmuseum.

25. John A Veverka, *The Interpretive Trails Book: Effective Planning and Design* (Edinburgh: MuseumsEtc, 2015).

5

Obstacled by Design

LIMITS FOR ACCESSIBILITY DEVELOPMENT

Accessibility is the right thing to do—as was stated by Janice Majewski and Lonnie Bunch back in 1998.[1] Although we have observed plenty of divergences in the actual practice, their intentions have, in theory, never been contradicted. There is a spectrum of possibilities in this field, from institutions with model accessibility proposals, to others that fail to achieve even minimum standards, to museums that have yet to apply the discipline altogether.

In museums, there is a striking gap between the expectations of this area (in terms of necessity, social justice, and potential) and its actual application. What is preventing the full deployment and development of accessibility and why? Why does this discipline often remain a confined subject? What explains the recurring inertia around this issue? Why do museums across the board often seem resistant to its full adoption?

Before trying to understand the existing contradictions, it is worth considering the historical tension between accessibility and preservation, which Robert R. Janes wrote about as early as 1995 in his book *Museums and the Paradox of Change*. To date, this and many other struggles do not seem to have made much headway. There has been little investigation into why accessibility is still considered a niche area and the field is perceived as difficult.

This resistance has sometimes come from those who do not have work experience in the accessibility sector, like curators, directors, or custodians who justify inaccessibility with trivial excuses: "No one has ever asked for them," or even, "We have never seen people who needed them." These are people whose responsibilities within their institutions include the subject matter but who are often unaware of the active potential of their role. In some cases, people can be hostile *a priori* for fear that accessibility might impede their activities. Since museum staff rarely, if ever, want to partake in social injustice, it can be difficult to talk openly about internal resistance. It is, however, important to recognize that latent opposition emerges from a series of results and considerations.

In this field, as in most, there is a paradoxical distance between theory and practice. Books, articles, newspapers, or social media often refer to an ideal context that hardly finds a concrete application in museum realities. We keep saying that accessibility is all we need, but in practice it does not happen. While there are exceptions, this distance is more perceivable in some contexts than in others. For example, this gap seems to be more significant in Italy compared to the United Kingdom. There are also different levels of awareness and policymaking within a single country where small-town museums can function differently compared to those in big cities.

All in all, the international debate on accessibility remains mainstream and at times superficial. It often lacks the force needed to break down prejudices and clichés that, on the outside, may not even appear problematic. What are the reasons behind this tendency? How can we raise awareness about accessibility more effectively?

The best-known hypothesis consists of elements like the lack of adequate training, limited staff diversity, or weak leadership support, but there are other latent issues at play. It is still considered taboo to talk about stereotypes associated with the topic, so these obstacles do not emerge frequently. These are certainly issues that can meet divergent opinions, but by analyzing certain methods and habits, it becomes clear how important it is to explicate these nodes.

FOR WHOM IS ACCESSIBILITY?

One of the most common definitions of accessibility is the act of removing barriers and enabling access to as many people as possible. Yet, in museums, existing strategies and approaches mostly concern people with disabilities: Are we sure this is the most correct and effective strategy? What indirect impacts does this approach generate, and, if any, what prejudices does it reveal?

To answer these central questions, we will need to take a couple steps back. People with disabilities, as often repeated in this volume, are those who risk encountering the most impassable barriers in museums, as well as in society at large. These obstacles must be knocked down, and to enable this to happen, museum staff need to acquire specific knowledge and skills. Moreover, we are not referring to the removal of—often essential—activities or proposals for this target audience, but rather to thinking about this discipline in a different and broader way.

As mentioned earlier in the book, this subject was born in response to a movement and its battles to obtain basic rights for this specific group, but certain definitions and labels might have crystalized the debate in a way that thwarts the field's evolution. For this reason, it may be necessary to bring into question some approaches traditionally upheld by this discipline: to support the construction of an accessible mentality, to apply this mentality more naturally and systematically, and to address some of the stereotypes that it may unintentionally generate toward people with disabilities. Erroneous perceptions of accessibility, in fact, may have a strong impact on the people to whom it is addressed. If we consider accessibility as something that only concerns people with disabilities, it sounds like they have more needs than others, instead of simply considering them different. This way of understanding disability can also appear paternalistic. When we look at people with disabilities as people who only need help, we undermine and penalize their autonomy. Access, most of the time, focuses only on disability with the risk of limiting the importance assigned to other characteristics—ranging from visitors' prior knowledge to their ages—that would be equally essential to deliver effective proposals.

Another taboo that often goes unaddressed is that accessibility is perceived as economically unsustainable, especially for smaller institutions with limited funding that might dismiss certain initiatives because they seem to address a limited audience. This kind of misunderstanding sometimes leaves museum workers demotivated, and they might limit their efforts, thinking that investing in accessibility benefits very few people. The mistake in this case resides at the root: both because inclusion by its very nature cannot always be based on a principle of sustainability, and because accessibility, as we have seen, often responds to needs common to many. It is necessary to start thinking about this discipline in a structured way to shift our focus and target a wider audience. There is a mistaken tendency to forget that disability is a condition that often occurs also with advancing age and in temporary or contingent ways: well-known elements of theory that we must integrate not only into our practice, but also into our perception of society.

REPRESENTATION ISSUES

There are stereotypes associated with disability that accessibility should help dismantle and not reinforce. Since accessibility relates closely to the quality of visitor experiences, the discipline can defer to well-established approaches used in the field of inclusive design. Furthermore, people committed to access need to defend and guarantee fair representation to ensure that disability is given well-deserved visibility.

This work must, therefore, address a number of prejudices. In most cases, these perceptions are not acquired through direct knowledge and can be easily found also in all other media, not just in the museum world.[2] For example, impairments are sometimes perceived as tragedies, or a person with a disability is identified as a heroic survivor.[3] People with disabilities, moreover, are often subject to "a form of 'benevolent prejudice' that expresses itself through the language of care, normality and likeness, and rejects an independent political identity for disabled people."[4]

In the seventies, the debate around these issues began insisting on the need to promote visibility and a more accurate representation. Since then, the message has remained constant, but the strategies of political action have changed, ranging from activist Mike Ervin's protest against Telethon and its "pietistic approach," as discussed in the 2005 documentary *The Kids Are All Right*,[5] to the Disability Visibility Project, an acclaimed series of podcasts dedicated to "recording, amplifying and sharing disability media and culture."[6]

In recent years, there has been a growing number of initiatives, often grassroots in nature, urging museums to question the existence of unique and exclusive histories, particularly in countries grappling with how to include different narratives. Incorrect or missing representation risks adding more to the preexisting barriers in museums and beyond.

Numerous studies conducted by the Research Centre for Museums and Galleries (RCMG) at the University of Leicester (UK) have shown how museums can contribute to social inclusion and foster equality through collections and exhibitions. They, indeed, have the power to change beliefs and perceptions. This shift starts with the choice of works to display and by directly involving diverse people—like people with disabilities—in rethinking interpretations and design solutions. The Access and Community Programs Education Department of the Metropolitan Museum of Art developed Crip the Met, "an initiative that engaged disability scholars and activists, curators, educators, and artists in discussion about representations of disability in the Museum, with the goal of developing interpretive guidelines for writing about disability and art."[7] User-centered experiences include users from the get-go.

It is quintessential to view disability not as an ontological characteristic, but as a set of fluid conditions that need to be understood through continuous and dynamic discourse. The difficulty lies at the origin, in conflict with a system more often charged with "bias against those who insist on calling people with disabilities 'special needs' and not considering them as patrons worthy of being reached."[8] These biases are difficult to unveil, and in most cases precede—and often undermine—the proper development of the accessible approach applied in the museum context. This is particularly evident in some proposals dedicated to art therapy, which applies a medical perspective and considers visitors "patients" and not "visitors." Or in those activities originally designed for children and offered to adults with cognitive disabilities: a choice that reinforces yet another stigma in which disability is associated with an infantile, docile, and even asexual dimension.

It is crucial to represent disability in order to restore a credible narrative of the world and question apparent standards of normalcy: "Visit any art gallery, see any film or play associated with disability, and watch a disabled provocateur like Mat Fraser totally mess with the head of a (non-disabled) audience—and you will see many theoretical messages conveyed."[9] In general, characterizing individuals exclusively by their condition contradicts people-first language, as we cannot consider a visitor with a disability only as a visitor with a disability. In other words, this target is often seen as problematic and remains a poorly studied group in museums, with the risk of developing a partial, and sometimes erroneous, representation. There are, however, some scholars and activists who believe that the problem is not

Chapter 5

rooted in representation or language choices, since these aspects are far removed from empirical research, are tied to an exclusively academic perspective, and veer from the ultimate goal of changing the dominant mentality.[10] No matter where one stands in the debate, the decision to adopt a certain lexicon or a particular path of visibility is a way to demonstrate an institution's awareness of the state of the art.

What emerges from this debate is that dealing with accessibility is always also a matter of representation, even in the choice to insist on inclusive design, in the quality of the adopted solutions, or in the role of aesthetics assigned to the projects. This is why it is also important to address, for instance, the role of aesthetics in given projects. Accessibility is often associated with unattractive initiatives, poor design, and unaesthetic tools. Even among those who deal with accessibility, some have insisted on placing this subject in opposition to aesthetics. This discourse reinforces a divergent and dangerous idea that appears throughout the history of the third sector in which associations or small organizations have often constituted an important support network, but conventionally have given little thought to the quality of their image.

In this sense, project planning promotes innovative research that allows disability and design to mutually influence each other and to foster new meanings.[11] More recently, the 2008 exhibition *Access+Ability*, set at the Cooper Hewitt in New York,[12] highlighted ways in which quality design simplifies users' lives without compromising the quality of form, and above all, avoids reinforcing stereotypes.

WHAT ARE BARRIERS?

Over the years, accessibility has broadened the scope of its interventions and the disciplines it covers. Initially focused on the removal of physical barriers, the discipline has expanded to include solutions to communication barriers and learning in general. The realm of expertise has become increasingly interdisciplinary and now includes law, architecture, special needs education, pedagogy, museology, environmental psychology, user design, digital studies, and many others. Accordingly, the type of intervention responds to a variety of domains and hypothetically covers all aspects of visitors' experiences. Yet many people who work in the field strictly focus on breaking down sensory, physical, and cognitive barriers, without considering the ones people face before they cross the threshold. Chapter 8 will return to this point in its discussion of cultural, economic, linguistic, technological, and other barriers.

In the recently published volume *Culture Is Bad for You*, Orian Brook, Dave O'Brien, and Mark Taylor analyze the intersections between race, class, and gender in the mechanisms of inequality within cultural and creative industries based on the findings of a large study conducted in the United Kingdom.[13] The authors address the lack of data as part of a general incomprehension of disability, and their research points to the system's inherent exclusiveness. This is especially true when it comes to identifying educational and occupational barriers that generate structural discrimination against this group of people.

When it comes to removing barriers to include people with disabilities, museums are missing barrier maps as well as articulated assessments of the quantity of obstacles and their locations: important prerequisites for problem-solving in this field. The fact that accessibility arises mostly from intuition or other models is full of good intentions but does not allow us to analyze the context in which to apply state-of-the-art criteria and propose the most relevant interventions. Improvisation does not allow us to see solutions that can sometimes be even simpler, and it gives the impression that accessibility lacks rigor and is inevitably expensive.

In reality, this last point is not always true. Expenses, which are, of course, relative to the institution's available resources, can certainly be high in the case of major interventions, but they can also be extremely low for minor actions that, within the framework of accurate planning, can prove valuable in improving the quality of what is on offer. The idea that accessibility results from expensive solutions marks yet another misunderstanding that overlooks the value of research and small experiments.

A particularly significant list, for example, is the one drawn up a few years ago by the Access Office at the Kennedy Center in Washington. It includes sixty low-cost solutions, all achievable under one hundred dollars, and it demonstrates what can be done if there is an awareness and a will to change things. They range from "providing visitors with magnifying glasses" to the suggestion of "making sure that staff introduce themselves, since it is not possible for everyone to recognize their uniforms."[14]

One of the most controversial questions explores the reality of limited access: Can everything really be made accessible, and at what cost? What are the conditions for exceptions? These questions frequently come up in the European debate on physical accessibility issues. On this continent, the historical, urban fabric often puts principles of conservation in opposition to those of accessibility, especially in smaller municipalities. These issues require complex responses. Certain experiences, like that of the British National Trust, indicate that wherever it is possible to install electricity, accessibility should not pose a problem, and architecture worldwide has shown how even historical buildings can become barrier-free spaces.[15] Clearly, there are borderline situations in which accessibility is not really possible, like at the Leaning Tower of Pisa, a famous site in Italy, to name just one. A more common example can be found at exhibitions with captions in English where people who do not understand this language cannot access the content. Institutions must try to break down as many barriers as possible with the awareness that accessibility is an active process in a given direction. In the cases in which it cannot be fully achieved, it is important to make explicit the presence of barriers and adopt alternative solutions. In situations like these, good practices also involve users and provide opportunities for ongoing dialogue. These suggestions are also useful as a reminder that this field requires specific skills and calls for interdisciplinary cooperation, and that the practice does not necessarily result in rigid, standardized provisions; it can offer scope for experimentation, especially in direct collaboration with recipients, even in apparently less accessible cases.

Museums are in the midst of a revolution that needs to find institutional footfall. They need to try to understand the advantages and disadvantages of potential access strategies, especially in the long term. Therefore, this work implies deep analysis and questions to reflect the complex reality of every context.

ASSUMING RESPONSIBLE FOR ACCESSIBILITY

In recent years, museum seats have been frequently used as a metaphor for explaining accessibility, with the risk, however, of keeping the focus on tools and aids over processes, approaches, and the organizational ramifications that accessibility implies. A lot depends on who is in charge of access and the space assigned to that function. Hence, there is a need for a professional figure whose job it is to usher access into museums at large. While, at present, accessibility is largely delegated to staff who are involved in educational activities, this dynamic is evident at international conferences on this topic.

US museums provide an exception to this rule through the figure of the accessibility coordinator, who is responsible, in some cases, for ensuring that people with disabilities are able to participate in all programs and activities. This figure, covered by the ADA and Section 504 of the Rehabilitation Act, helps single organizations to fully comply with their legal requirements, and not only in the area of education.[16] Additional responsibilities include educating staff, spearheading access programs, and crafting an access statement.[17] What is interesting to note in these indications is that while this position can be delegated to an individual or a group of individuals, it should not be tied to any one department only, as it requires that accessibility take on a systemic dimension.[18]

At museums that do not need to comply with this set of regulations and in other countries, it is no coincidence that educational activities represent a point of reference for accessibility. Moreover, each museum is characterized by its own organizational dynamics; only larger structures tend to hire an accessibility coordinator or even establish a dedicated department, one that is typically related to the educational one.[19] While it has been argued that the duties of this role can be shared among a group of volunteers, today we know that this solution is never desirable.

More generally, we can see that the educational services are more involved in accessibility than other areas that nevertheless interact with the public, like curatorship, exhibition management, or even custodial services. For example, exhibitions do not always involve experts on accessibility in the reflection on this topic. With regard to disability and the so-called *educational turn* that has taken place in curatorial practices in recent years, Amanda Cachia ponders ways of promoting the joint work of curators and educators so they can create experiences that are not only meaningful and accessible, but also capable of visibly reflecting on representation issues.[20]

In their book about exhibition design, Polly McKenna-Cress and Janet Kamien highlight the benefits of a collaborative approach and associate accessibility with the work of the designer, who "must ensure that the exhibition experience is comfortable, engaging, memorable, and ultimately meaningful."[21] Tiina Roopola agrees that the designer's work best meets the criteria of complex design that can offer mediation to meet diverse human needs, though she laments the lack of intellectual recognition of the profession and specific training opportunities in the museum field.[22]

There is an evident push toward progressive cross-functional integration of roles and skills, even if in practice this trend does not always result in cooperation between different internal functions. In most cases, accessibility remains somewhat circumscribed, and not all staff feel the responsibility to master the subject matter in a meaningful way. A clear exception can be found in small institutions where one person performs several tasks within the museum. However, in such cases accessibility is even more rarely considered an institutional priority.

It is surprising to see that accessibility is sometimes adopted only at the surface. This is especially evident in museums that host highly skilled accessibility departments but that do not live up to the same standards when designing exhibitions. This tends to occur when colleagues make choices without consulting other staff members who have more experience with accessibility. The lack of coherence between different departments suggests there is a broken link along the chain of communication, a dynamic that has a negative impact on the institution's image.

INSIDE THE ORGANIZATION

To generate visible and concrete impacts, accessibility needs to be part of ground operations, especially on the organizational level. Widespread and structured training is an important start. It is important to diversify personnel and to cultivate leadership that is willing to make accessibility a central part of museum work. The second part of this book will explore these suggestions in greater depth.

Accessibility is not yet a topic whose knowledge is widely disseminated in museums. One of the key issues to consider is undoubtedly that of training, from the lack of dedicated university courses to the irregularity of professional and continuing education proposals. In this sense, the quality of training makes a big difference. Accessibility training needs to sensitize museum staff to the pitfalls associated with patronizing approaches and to confer critical tools, like the capacity to evaluate its accessibility measures and the ways in which staff and audiences perceive them.

The disciplinary narrowness that access is subject to limits its transformative contribution and effectiveness. While it is fundamental to impart skills, like how to facilitate the tactile exploration of an object or how to relate to people with disabilities, these teachings cannot be considered sufficient to take on new relevance in the organization. Today, dealing with this subject requires design and facilitation skills, team-management skills, and problem-solving qualities, not to mention specific awareness associated with the needs of different audiences. In addition, best practices suggest the need for ongoing training, not only for those who specialize in this area, but for all staff. In fact, overall effectiveness can fail due to a lack of alignment between the quality of the offerings and its communication.

Staff homogeneity is, without doubt, another limiting element that impinges on an institution's ability to welcome and listen to different needs. A museum in which the staff is not diverse, especially at the managerial and leadership level, will undoubtedly find it more difficult to develop suitably diverse solutions. Moreover, this issue raises the question of representation: Only by diversifying the staff can one hope to diversify the public.

Diversification should avoid targeting limited groups and support broad-ranging connections between different areas. With a focus on disability, Marcus Weisen considers "the absence or insufficient joint work between departments" to be one of the determining circumstances of inaccessibility. This observation emerges from his list of factors causing intellectual inaccessibility in British museums, written over ten years ago.[23] Many of his considerations, however, are still relevant today and apply specifically to accessibility: They include "weak institutional commitment to disability equality, poor awareness of legal duties [and] no collection of information on best practice," as well as the involvement of disabled people being delayed or carried out "in a token way."[24]

To reverse these trends, we need the full support of people in leadership because decision-makers catalyze transformation. Many experiences teach us that only museums whose leadership is committed to the creation of an accessible culture can implement lasting and effective projects. From this point of view, we cannot fail to note that the numerous books published in recent years about changes in museum work have consistently identified the centrality of this aspect and encouraged greater opportunities for an inclusive leadership style with the ability to eschew stereotypes and prejudices, preventing their propagation. For this to happen, it will be necessary to promote accessibility first and foremost as an ingrained mindset, and not as a set of prepackaged solutions. Access is a long-sighted process that involves museum structures in their entirety.

NOTES

1. Janice Majewski and Lonnie Bunch, "The Expanding Definition of Diversity: Accessibility and Disability Culture Issues in Museum Exhibitions," *Curator* 41, no. 3 (1998), https://doi.org/10.1111/j.2151-6952.1998.tb00829.x.
2. Richard Sandell, Jocelyn Dodd, and Rosemarie Garland-Thomson, eds., *Re-Presenting Disability: Activism and Agency in the Museum* (London: Routledge, 2013), 95.
3. Ibid.
4. Jocelyn Dodd, Richard Sandell, Debbie Jolly, and Ceri Jones, *Rethinking Disability Representation in Museums and Galleries: Supporting Papers* (Leicester: Research Centre for Museums and Galleries [RCMG], University of Leicester, 2013), 45, https://

le.ac.uk/-/media/uol/docs/research-centres/rcmg/publications/rethinking-dis
ability-representation-supporting-papers.pdf.
5. *The Kids Are All Right*, accessed May 1, 2021, http://www.thekidsareallright.org/.
6. Disability Visibility Project, accessed May 1, 2021, https://disabilityvisibilityprojec
t.com.
7. "Annual Report for the Year 2018–2019," the Metropolitan Museum of Art, accessed
June 17, 2021, https://www.metmuseum.org/-/media/files/about-the-met/annu
al-reports/2018-2019/annual-report-2018-19.pdf?la=en&hash=CA4A390302E
D38ACB2EB9ACEBB7B80E6.
8. Cathy Kudlick and Edward M. Luby, "Access as Activism: Bringing the Museum to
the People," in *Museums and Activism*, ed. Robert Janes and Richard Sandell (London:
Routledge, 2019).
9. Dan Goodley, *Disability Studies: An Interdisciplinary Introduction*, 2nd ed. (Thousand
Oaks, CA: SAGE, 2017), loc. 249 of 1285, Kindle.
10. Tom Shakespeare, *Disabilità e società. Diritti, falsi miti, percezioni sociali* (Trento: Erikson, 2017).
11. Graham Pulling, *Design Meets Disability* (Cambridge, MA: MIT Press, 2009).
12. The *Access + Ability* exhibition was on display at the Cooper Hewitt, Smithsonian
Design Museum in New York, from December 15, 2017, to September 3, 2018.
More information is available online at https://www.cooperhewitt.org/channel/
access-ability.
13. Orian Brook, Dave O'Brien, and Mark Taylor, *Culture Is Bad for You: Inequality in the
Cultural and Creative Industries* (Manchester: Manchester University Press, 2020).
14. "Accessibility for Under 100 Dollars," Oregon Arts Commission, accessed February
23, 2021, https://www.oregonartscommission.org/publications-and-resources/ac
cessibility-under-100-dollars.
15. "The National Trust: Involving Disabled Users in Designing Access Features Can Be
Transformative," Disability Arts International, accessed February 23, 2021, https://
www.disabilityartsinternational.org/resources/the-national-trust-involving-dis
abled-users-in-designing-access-features-can-be-transformative/.
16. In the case of the ADA, Title II includes the designation of a "responsible employee"
who is called upon to enforce accessibility constraints.
17. National Endowment for the Arts, *Accessibility Planning and Resource Guide for
Cultural Administrators*, 2011, accessed February 23, 2021, https://www.arts.gov/
impact/accessibility/publications-checklists-and-resources/accessibility-plan
ning-and-resource-guide-cultural-administrators.
18. Heather J. L. Smith, Barry Gingley, and Hanna Goodwin, "Beyond Compliance? Museums, Disability and the Law," in *Museums, Equality and Social Justice,* eds. Richard
Sandell and Eithne Nightingale (London: Routledge, 2012), 59–71.
19. As suggested in the United States by the National Endowment for the Arts and the
American Alliance of Museums.
20. Amanda Cachia, "Disability, Curating and the Educational Turn: The Contemporary Condition of Access in the Museum," *On-Curating*, Issue 24, 2014, https://
www.on-curating.org/issue-24-reader/disability-curating-and-the-educational
-turn-the-contemporary-condition-of-access-in-the-museum.html#.YTng-
w9OA4-R.

21. Polly McKenna-Cress and Janet Kamien, *Creating Exhibitions: Collaboration in the Planning, Development, and Design of Innovative Experiences* (Hoboken, NJ: Wiley, 2013), 133.
22. Tiina Roppola, *Designing for the Museum Visitor Experience* (New York: Routledge, 2011). Kindle.
23. Marcus Weisen, "From the Margins to the Core?" in *Sackler Conference for Arts Education* (Wednesday, March 24 to Friday, March 26, 2010), accessed March 2, 2021, http://media.vam.ac.uk/media/documents/conferences/2010/margins-to-the-core/v&a-fromthemarginstothecore-compiledpapers&notes.pdf.
24. Ibid.

6

Accessibility as a Strategic and Systemic Process

Professionals and researchers have debated about the traditional definition of *accessibility* and the field's development in recent years, questioning whom the discipline addresses and new methodologies to adopt. There is a slow transformation underway, but it is tinged by ambiguity. For one, it has always claimed to be "for everyone" without clearly specifying its recipients. Secondly, museums are encouraged to be more inclusive, but activities geared toward access will not penetrate the institution's ecosystem, and lastly, they embrace access as a revolutionary process but without framing it within a long-term strategy.

In short, there are many challenges ahead of us, and these require a cultural transformation regarding organizational and policy levels. As a discipline, accessibility needs to reflect on its methods and original aspirations. It accompanies visitors throughout their lives and responds to people's needs thanks to its power to dismantle social prejudices through the adoption of new methods and forms of knowledge.

INCLUSIVE DESIGN

For accessibility to become a prerequisite for any project, our focus must turn away from impairments and refocus on needs. This inclusive approach frees people from labels, helping to change a dangerous concept of "normality." By considering needs as permanent, temporary, or contingent,[1] we can conceive spaces and services as user-oriented and dismantle the paradox that accessibility is a niche topic.

Redefining the scale of operations to favor an open and fluid use allows us to consider the dynamic nature of our societies, as well as that of people: Our constituents are in constant flux.[2] The purpose of this reversal is also to insist on the creation of fully accessible museums rather than places where accessibility is an option limited in space and time that does not guarantee visitors' autonomy. As mentioned earlier, this habitual approach threatens to reinforce a wrong perception of disability itself, emphasizing prescribed differences that may not reflect people's actual diversity. According to some authors, like the anthropologist Francesco Remotti, to bring individuals closer together, it is necessary to insist on their similarities within fluid identities that allow us to recognize ourselves.[3] This implies approaching access recipients in broad and multifaceted ways and not only on the basis of characteristics that fit a fixed grid. We do not know people with disabilities, just as we don't know anyone except (perhaps) ourselves. We can identify some of their needs and find appropriate solutions, but it is extremely important not to freeze individual complexity behind single adjectives.

Inclusive Design aligns with this new understanding of accessibility very closely and has the merit of facilitating social interaction and inclusion wherever this is possible. It also recognizes that some situations call for more protected and exclusive context, as we discussed earlier. This approach can devise solutions that are suitable for each recipient in virtue of the fact that they are based on deep listening, based on a principle aimed at understanding user diversity. It differentiates itself from Universal Design, albeit with frequent misunderstandings, which sanctions single solutions as universally valid for many. This paradigm is founded on the principle of fair use, as it harbors the expectation that all users are offered the same experience, without segregating or stigmatizing anyone with special arrangements or the need to ask for them. These brief considerations shine light on how accessibility represents a very different set of ideas that can, by contrast, be easily integrated into the field of Inclusive Design in order to facilitate "the creation of experiences that are not only compliant with standards, but truly usable and open to all."[4]

In this regard, Sina Bahram of Prime Access Consulting recalls how both Universal and Inclusive Design "address the big picture," while accessibility consists of "those things we do specifically for those with functional differences."[5] The expert underlines how the attempt to break the association between accessibility and disability by trying to include "the widest possible audience" has been considered not only by museums but also in all other sectors.[6] According to the reflections of this and other authors, the word *accessibility* sometimes seems inadequate to fully address needs that need further expansion. This leaves us with two options: to assign new meanings to the word *accessibility* or to adopt new terms. The proposal to rethink the recipients in light of their complexities, whatever these may be, reinforces the principle that diversity is the only true recurring characteristic of each person. In fact, it draws on our similarities. The reference to diversity in this sense alludes to "all the people and differences among us" rather than the "specific characteristics of only the minority within a group of people or in society."[7] Diversity becomes the real resource of a museum, for the types of solutions it incentivizes, the target groups it involves, and the staff it invites, especially when this variety of perspectives enhances creativity.

Accessibility can be seen as a space of inquiry, one that becomes invisible through its perfect integration, becoming the starting point for understanding different people with different needs through different solutions (when needed). It poses a complex and far-from-easy challenge but remains a worthwhile investment of time and trust.

ACCESSIBILITY AS A PROCESS

Systems thinking in museums offers a great opportunity for envisioning accessibility under a different light. Ann Rowson Love and Yuha Jung describe certain ideas and experiences in reference to a collaborative organizational structure in which authority is shared and able to generate strong community engagement.[8] Systems thinking is a method, but above all a mindset. It indicates new ways of looking at accessibility as more than a bundle of incremental, single solutions, but as a framework of shared processes occurring on several levels and oriented toward a long-term set of objectives.

Similar reflections aimed at promoting a process of change in museums come from parallel disciplines, namely design. From this point of view, it is not surprising to find this drive already in 1988 in John Salmen's considerations delivered to the then American Association of Museums (now the American Alliance of Museums).[9] The author, a user-experience designer, wrote *Everyone's Welcome: The Americans with Disabilities Act and Museums*, in response to the legislative act, and his reflections are still relevant today. It provides a strategic approach to the subject and presents examples that explain aspects of the American Disability Act (ADA) that mostly relate to museums, supporting "programs and structures that are fully accessible at every level."[10] The second part of the volume is especially notable because of "The Nine Building Blocks to Accessibility," a step-by-step guide "that museums may use to evaluate, plan, implement, and advertise accessibility at their sites."[11] This text puts forth the following recommendations with reference to the ADA's Title II and III:

1. Include a statement committing to accessibility in the museum's general policy or mission statement;
2. Designate an accessibility coordinator, either an individual or a group;
3. Obtain input from people with disabilities;
4. Organize an Accessibility Advisory Council of people with disabilities;
5. Train staff on accessibility, the ADA, and strategies for serving all visitors;
6. Conduct a review of facilities and programs to identify existing barriers and discriminatory policies or practices;
7. Implement short- and long-term institution-wide accessibility, including program accessibility, barrier removal, effective communication, and new construction and alterations;
8. Promote and advertise accessibility in the museum;

9.   Establish a grievance process;
10. Conduct an ongoing review of accessibility efforts.[12]

Salmen explicitly states that the full adoption of all nine points may not be necessary, especially in small organizations. For institutions of all sizes, however, this framework remains an excellent model for introducing or implementing accessibility, bearing recipients in mind from the outset of the design process.

This operation-oriented approach finds similar developments at other organizations, like the National Endowment for the Arts, which published significant handbooks already in 2003 and in 2011.[13] In the United Kingdom, the Museums, Library, Archives Council (MLA)[14] developed a series of suggestions that share a similar intent with the American ones but differ in the approach.[15] The British solution intends "to help museums, libraries and archives to develop an understanding of their current practice and to encourage positive developments in relation to a variety of key issues."[16] This guide for self-evaluation is entitled *Access for All Self-Assessment Toolkit*, available online.[17] It stands out for its focus on aspects instrumental to a structured adoption of the discipline, including staff training, employment, and consultation and feedback.

These documents all offer schemes for the evaluation and self-analysis of internal processes, providing in-depth guidance useful to most organizations. They focus primarily on disability issues, but their approaches can be recalibrated more broadly to issues of Diversity, Equity, Access, and Inclusion (DEAI) and accessibility as a whole.

Imagining that this subject could cross an entire organization requires a figure who is able to coordinate and manage the process. In this sense, it is necessary to work on training, communication, and organizational charts capable of assigning functions and guaranteeing the full cooperation of those who deal with accessibility. This passage also means that whoever oversees this matter should assume the role of a project manager and not be seen as a mere educator, both for reasons of role recognition and scope of responsibilities. As seen, this function is already present in those contexts where a similar figure is required by law, but in the given case refers to a figure who is not prescribed by legislative applications but deals with design in the broadest sense of the term. This does not mean eliminating this competence from the field of education, but rather reinforcing different interdisciplinary processes that lie beyond this field.

At its source, this process is even more complex: It will require a restructuring of the matter so that it becomes a shared responsibility and part of a solid, clearly defined development process. In fact, only accessibility conceived in this way becomes a strategic resource founded on the whole institution's knowledge.

Generally speaking, pathways that rely exclusively on the sensitivity of a few individuals within the institution are fragile. People change roles and jobs, thereby interrupting a chain of relationships and awareness. Any choice made in the long run must be part of a long-term plan supported by an institution's leaders.

TO SUM UP

In order for accessibility to find its own effective formulation, there are several key cultural and procedural assumptions that need to be recognized. First of all, it is necessary to consider the following prerequisites for structured accessibility:

- A full commitment from leadership and decision-makers who consider accessibility a common goal to be shared at all levels;
- Training and ongoing professional development of all staff including leaders, decision-makers, employees, and volunteers;
- Willingness to actively involve recipients and stakeholders in the design, but especially in the evaluation and testing processes;
- Financial, time, and human resources.

Once these aspects have been put in place, accessibility can take a new course to become effective and partially free from the perceptions and constraints to which it is subject. Only then can the discipline adopt new approaches. Many of these have already appeared in the discussion thus far, but it still may be useful to offer a brief summary:

1. We need to start from needs and not from labels. This means taking an honest look at the needs museums do not meet. Starting from those, we can propose visitor-centered initiatives that include as many people as possible;
2. It is essential to analyze barriers, not only those associated with disability, but all barriers in general. The most widespread obstacles are cultural and cognitive by nature. Many people who are not used to attending museums feel inadequate in these spaces and are unable to understand contents that remain distant from their life experience. We must become aware of barriers that prevent participation in the first place like the lack of habit, along with barriers to education and professional growth. All of these barriers can also intersect with disability;
3. In terms of the process, it is important to start with an analysis of all barriers *before* developing solutions. Barriers can be found in all areas of production from communication to digital resources, from venue staff to events and even educational activities;
4. Access needs structured, integrated interventions that define new areas of internal collaboration. We need to adopt shared guidelines, imagine processes, communicate internally and externally, carefully train staff, redefine the organizational plan, and adopt clear policies, using an ecosystemic model in which everything is interconnected;
5. It is essential to avoid rhetoric that distinguishes "us" and "them," remembering that organizations should ensure equal access and opportunities. One must be careful not to create stereotypes by emphasizing the differences between

in-groups and out-groups. We must remember that inclusion is not philanthropy and that people have their own tastes, interests, and desires that must always be respected, even in their choice not to attend cultural venues, even when these are perfectly accessible.

This series of considerations offers cues for a broader reflection on the theme of accessibility. These approaches have proven effective through decades of individual projects, cases, and experiences. On a practical level, we see that they have been adopted by a new culture in the world of design, but much less so in museums. In fact, when these aspects are not fulfilled, we see a progressive diffusion of proposals that act on a surface level, usually through the adoption of minimum standards or sporadic initiatives that cannot be considered adequate measures for a museum that wants to call itself accessible. Opportunities for success lie within a structure-wide approach with an impact-based perspective. It is defined by inclusive, high-quality design and, above all, cross-checked phases and a solid foundation in the organizational structure.

Another aim of this positive-feedback system is the development of a "learning organization" in the sense of a group of people that is "able to create, acquire and share knowledge and to use this knowledge to modify that behavior."[18] Having a clear institutional understanding of this need is perhaps the first objective to keep in mind, first and foremost through training. The next part of this book will walk through these developmental phases step by step to help organizations become more inclusive.

NOTES

1. Kat Holmes, *Mismatch: How Inclusion Shapes Design* (Cambridge: The MIT Press, 2018).
2. Edward Steinfeld and Jordana Maisel, *Universal Design: Creating Inclusive Environments* (Hoboken, NJ: Wiley, 2012), 51.
3. Francesco Remotti, *Somiglianze: Una via per la convivenza* (Bari: Laterza, 2020).
4. Holmes, *Mismatch*, 55.
5. Sina Bahram, "The Inclusive Museum," in *The Senses: Design Beyond Vision*, eds. Ellen Lupton and Andrea Lipps (New York: Princeton Architectural Press, 2018), 25–26.
6. Ibid.
7. Tina C. Nielsen and Lisa Kepinski, *Inclusion Nudges for Motivating Allies in All Organizations and Communities* (Self-published, 2020).
8. Yuha Jung and Ann Rowson Love, eds., *Systems Thinking in Museums: Theory and Practice* (Lanham, MD: Rowman & Littlefield, 2017).
9. The American Association of Museums is now called the American Alliance of Museums.
10. John P. S. Salmen, *Everyone's Welcome: The Americans with Disabilities Act and Museums* (Washington, DC: American Association of Museums, 1998), 4, https://files.eric.ed.gov/fulltext/ED437754.pdf.

11. Ibid., 34.
12. Ibid., 35. In the original text, the ADA requirement from the Title II—State and Local Government—are indicated with a star and correspond to points 1, 2, 3, 5, 6 (partially), 8, and 9, while those related to Title III—Public Accommodation and Services Operated by Private Organizations—correspond to points 6 (partially) and 9.
13. National Endowment for the Arts, *Design for Accessibility: A Cultural Administrators Handbook*, 2003, accessed March 2, 2021, https://www.arts.gov/sites/default/files/Design-for-Accessibility.pdf; National Endowment for the Arts, *Accessibility Planning and Resource Guide for Cultural Administrators*, 2011, accessed March 2, 2021, https://www.arts.gov/sites/default/files/AccessibilityPlanningAll.pdf.
14. The Museums, Library, Archives Council (MLA) was dismantled in 2012, and its functions were subsumed by the Arts Council England.
15. The Museums, Libraries and Archives Council, *Access for All Self-Assessment Toolkit: Checklist 1, Disability Access for Museums, Libraries and Archives*, January 8, 2006, 4, www.nemo.org/fileadmin/Dateien/public/topics/Disability_and_museums/disability_checklist_pdf_6540.pdf.
16. Ibid.
17. Ibid.
18. Robert R. Janes, *Museums and the Paradox of Change*, 3rd ed. (London: Routledge, 2013).

Part II
Cultivating Organizational Change

In this part of the book, we will explore concrete recommendations designed to initiate a process of change—in mentality, skill sets, and values—through a series of training sessions related to the systemic and processual nature of accessibility. Building on the theoretical overview put forth in the first half of the book, this ongoing journey views accessibility much like a design discipline that leverages a museum's potential to transform step by step. The first stage involves defining a vision from which an institution can assess objectives. By sticking to small, concrete actions, institutional change can feel clear-cut and doable without shying away from the complexities of the process. These next chapters introduce a series of tools and solutions that help set a foundation for real design. Aptitudes like listening and co-design will be key in the development of the process.

From a procedural point of view, accessibility rarely receives the attention it deserves. It is first and foremost a process. Its development is implicit to medium- and long-term planning and its proposals, like the definition of strategic plans for accessibility, a mandatory output in light of this discussion. This approach stretches the boundaries of the discipline well beyond the confines of museum education. It takes its cues from the practice of design thinking as a set of cognitive, strategic, and practical processes that accompany the development of a product or service.

Design thinking has been used frequently in several cultural institutions because it helps us understand people's needs and motivations. In the long term, this method stimulates innovative ideas and solutions. This discussion draws inspiration from its five phases: empathize, define, ideate, prototype, and test. Herein, these steps offer a frame of reference and are not intended as a strict sequence. In recent years, this kind of approach has also boosted audience development strategies, enabling cultural organizations to reach new audiences and strengthen their relationship with existing ones. Along the same lines as practices outlined in this book, a British Council toolkit from 2016 can help guide an organization through audience development, including the following considerations:

1. It involves an attitude and a philosophy that look outward; it values visitors while tending to a set of tools;
2. It does not make any assumptions about visitors, but solicits their study and observation;
3. It encompasses everything you do, from exhibition planning and education activities to publicity campaigns;
4. It considers all the details, aware that small things can make a big difference;
5. It is not just a one-off project; it is ongoing.

A variety of methods inform the second half of the book, but the whole process follows a general arc. The first step is to make a plan and to define objectives. Then the team needs to examine barriers and outline solutions with the help of internal and external stakeholders. The last step is an in-depth evaluation to test the process in order to define and implement practices that lead to policymaking.

Each of the following chapters consists of two parts: a theoretical introduction to the topic illustrated with examples and case studies, followed by a second section with practical ideas for training. The first part will allow the reader to delve deeper into topics that have only been touched on thus far, and which constitute essential phases in the planning process. The second part stems from the need to disseminate new content to help organizations design an accessibility plan suitable to their size and scale through practical exercises. These training exercises are not intended to replace more traditional courses designed to build awareness of disabilities. These require their own, in-depth studies. This set of exercises are intended as a complement to such work. These reflections are designed to promote a new mentality in which the needs of people are rightly understood in their specificities, while becoming systematically engrained in a broader discourse about accessibility.

The overarching purpose of the training and the conversations recommended here differs from that of many courses on these issues. The aim here is not so much to condemn existing levels of discrimination, but to encourage the adoption of proactive solutions, fueled by a keen desire to learn and improve, without dwelling on guilt. It is important to understand whether the training participants all work within a single museum or come from different institutions. This said, the suggested solutions can be adapted to suit both cases, and the number of participants can range from six to a hundred people, as long as different activities are created to ensure everyone's engagement. In general, the following activities are designed for about twenty to twenty-five people in a physical setting, but they can also be effectively carried out online, provided that certain arrangements are made. In this case, you will need not only programs like Zoom but also facilitation platforms like Jamboard, Padlet, and Miro, which support accessibility in many ways.

In general, the proposed workshops can last between four and six hours, which is not too long and still allows for effective content sharing. The agenda, with few exceptions, includes an introduction, an icebreaker, a presentation, and an activity that allows for reworking content and a final debriefing. Any workshop should begin with a general introduction that highlights the objectives and key questions to be addressed throughout the session, to offer an outline of the day's agenda. At this stage, when required, it is also helpful to give each participant something that immediately signals their assigned group. It is fun to use easily distinguishable cards that take on different shapes and colors. Alternatively, random groups can be formed, perhaps during icebreakers. In any case, these options will streamline later phases in group definition. The choice of icebreaker should be made based on the objectives, the number of participants, their needs, and the extent to which they know each other.

During such meetings, it is essential to conduct training in the most accessible way possible. Many ideas will be expressed implicitly, but it will be necessary to ensure that communication reaches everyone effectively and that everyone has the opportunity to listen and to express themselves. This principle also applies to presentations through the use of well-contrasted colors and minimal text, with visible and meaningful content accompanied by high-quality and relevant images. Moreover, the content of the slides should always be described briefly, and if needed, it would be worth assessing the possibility of involving a sign language interpreter and/or CART captioners. The presentation, in addition, should be shared in advance for those who might need to have it in printed form. At the end of each workshop it is the responsibility of the facilitator to transcribe all the contributions that have emerged and return them in the form of a report.

Regarding the target audience, it is important to involve colleagues with different roles, from educators to custodians, curators to exhibition managers, directors to volunteers. During the training, it is important that everyone has a chance to understand better and to envision their responsibilities and tasks. The activities proposed in the various meetings, in fact, do not only serve as exercises but also allow organizers to collect real information. If processed correctly, this data can contribute to development of accessibility in a given museum and facilitate collaboration with partner institutions.

Lastly, it is important to consider the decision-making power of participants within their own organizations, especially when the process is bottom-up and still needs to gain the support of leadership. If the staff is not in a position of responsibility, it will be appropriate to further enhance the training session with some practical suggestions to help increase the participants' sense of agency, empowering them to initiate real change from the ground up.

The second half of this book can be broken down as follows. Chapter 7 discusses the planning process and encourages a series of reflections to make *before* taking action. Chapter 8 examines barrier mapping as a key phase of accessibility development; this work implies more than removing barriers and requires a close analysis of the context, establishing priorities, and devising a timeline. Chapter 9 focuses on the need to involve internal and external allies in the development process, an essential step for any organization looking to promote inclusion through co-design. Chapter 10 is devoted to solutions: How do we go about achieving accessibility? There are plenty of good practices that serve as examples, while many are yet to be tested in terms of tools, process, and organization strategies. Chapter 11 explores evaluation strategies so as to gather useful information for the implementation of a strategic plan. The book concludes with reflections about the future of the discipline in chapter 12.

7

Establishing Your Process

As with any project, the first step in tackling accessibility is planning. We must take time to understand its context and visualize both the objectives and the whole journey before taking action. The project cycle must, therefore, begin with an analysis of the present, in the light of which it will then be possible to redefine the initial objectives with greater precision. The most common mistake, in fact, is to launch into the process without focusing on a direction that needs to be made up of different stages and oriented toward precise goals. The only way to approach accessibility efficiently is to develop a carefully thought-through course of action, invested with all the discipline's complexity. By envisioning the path, museum leaders can begin processing legitimate doubts or concerns and lay them to rest, an important step before getting the entire institution on board for the duration of the project.

The first task is an assessment of the current situation. It is a gateway that marks the transition from theory into practice. We need to remember that we are never starting from scratch: The current level of awareness and motivation helps us gauge preexisting conditions. Based on this premise, asking questions can translate into an opportunity for change: envisioning an idea so as to initiate action. This step can unveil dreams as well as unresolved challenges within an organization. The difficulty involved should not deter planners from being ambitious and reaching for the highest level of accessibility. This process also needs to empower staff and demonstrate the discipline's central importance. In this regard, it is worth repeating that many countries worldwide have legal obligations to provide and maintain accessibility, especially for visitors with disabilities, a factor that provides a clearer template for the standards that must be met. In such cases, the top priority is to ensure hasty compliance with regulations.

Whether you are working within a preestablished framework, or are lacking specific guidance, it can be hard to know where to start. Some suggest creating affiliations with local organizations, others recommend the use of self-assessment checklists, but neither scenario outlines a detailed process to follow. This is why this section of the book opens with the premise that planning is the first step in a process that includes: envisioning change, defining goals and understanding context, and visualizing the role of leadership and that of the whole institution. Organizations of all sizes can share this method and foster a common aspiration. Throughout the text, there will be suggestions tailored to small- to medium-sized institutions rather than to museums with a staff of over a hundred employees. Yet the approach, and especially the motivations, remain the same in each case.

ENVISIONING THE CHANGE AND THE STEPS TO REACH IT

When an organization decides to prioritize the role of accessibility, it results in placing people's needs at the center of the institution, and, even more importantly, it sets a process of change in motion. Organizations are often plagued by inertia, a shortage of resources, or an overwhelming workload. Short-term goals often drive them, and operations are split by an array of different values. Guiding them toward a new outlook is a strategic choice in a complex system. By visualizing the way in which certain goals can fit into a complex system of organizational needs, we can motivate people to embark on this challenging, but gratifying path. Research and benchmarking are other essential steps in imagining accessibility development. It is also important to illustrate how much positive impact best practices have had in other museums, so as to demonstrate the feasibility of this process.

This vision is also helpful to calm fears and reassure decision-makers who may worry about the scarcity of time and resources or those who are concerned that museums may lose sight of their original objectives. This fear is often accompanied by the misconception that cultural content might be trivialized. Some believe that very expensive technology is the only solution. Others worry that long-term planning is a waste of time. These ideas all underestimate the power of accessibility.

In short, building a vision for the future means motivating an organization to embark on a road forward, focusing on evidence-based needs. In this way, the new vision works together with a defined plan, allowing us to imagine the future we want to create and to identify the tools and thought process needed to get there. When the goals in question relate to accessibility, our top priority must be to ensure equal opportunities for different audiences to participate in museum activities. This aspiration, however valid, lacks the specificity for it to be fully achievable in the immediate future. We must define goals that consider multiple factors and meet SMART criteria (Specific, Measurable, Attainable, Relevant, and Time-Bound). This means that the information needed to precisely define goals will have to be gathered along the way, starting with context analysis and then the mapping of barriers. Goals may be small and intermediate or larger and more ambitious, but they should always exist within a broader, written strategy—one to be shared with colleagues—which takes a medium- to long-term look at the process.

What does accessibility mean *to us*? How do we expect our audience to change in the next two, five, or ten years? How do we plan to strengthen the relationship with existing visitors? What untapped audience do we want to reach? How can our museum make a difference? Are we ready for change? What risks do we run? What resources (economic, human, time, expertise) are we lacking, and how can we get them? How will we measure success? These are just a few of the questions it may be useful to ask before beginning this work, providing a foundation that will evolve over time, but will nonetheless serve as a common point of reference.

CONTEXT ANALYSIS

For any institution (large or small), context analysis is a fundamental step to gain insight into the existing level of awareness and to determine an institution's strengths and weaknesses. This sort of investigation allows us to gauge the extent to which accessibility is already regarded as an essential issue. Context analysis should be developed with clear objectives and must examine a number of different levels through appropriate research methods. Some of the most important aspects to consider incorporate:

- Activities in place and actions already carried out to date, in favor of accessibility and previously removed barriers;
- Levels of interest, attention, and awareness across all areas of the organization with regard to these issues;
- Types of recipients involved until now, especially those with specific needs and their feedback.

Understanding the present situation is an essential prerequisite for imagining future developments. This can also be supplemented by a broader self-assessment on general issues like leadership involvement and readiness or, for example, the existence of appropriate policies and staff training. Self-assessment provides the opportunity to identify areas that need improvement before venturing into the planning process; these developments require ongoing monitoring.

While museums conventionally relegate this field of practice to the education department, accessibility can be and ought to be expanded to all areas of an institution. Here is a basic outline of core issues with initial questions to consider:

- *Education*: Are all educational activities based on the assumptions of accessibility? Is the entire educational staff knowledgeable about these issues? What are the relationships between the education department and other areas of planning and audience development?
- *Leadership and mission*: How relevant are different needs and accessibility issues considered at the leadership level? Does the mission include accessibility? What does accessibility mean in this context?

- *Policy/management*: What does success look like in terms of accessibility? Do medium- to long-term strategies already include accessibility? Is there someone in charge of accessibility? What are their responsibilities? Do they have decision-making power and the capacity to coordinate between interdisciplinary functions?
- *Collection and interpretation*: To what extent does interpretation follow an interdisciplinary approach aimed at greater accessibility? Do collections include different stories and representation?
- *Staff training*: Does the whole staff receive regular training on accessibility?
- *Communication*: Does internal/external communication support equality? Does communication reach different recipients effectively? Are those persons involved in communications kept up-to-date on current activities and existing proposals?
- *Employment and human resources*: Does the museum actively recruit different employees and people at all levels?
- *Consultations and evaluation*: Is the museum in touch with different organizations for planning and evaluation? Is evaluation part of an ongoing implementation process? Does the museum periodically consult with different users to test its proposals? Is there an accessibility reference committee?

Each one of these questions deserves in-depth examination, demonstrating how the entire organization needs to work together to successfully become accessible. The whole community plays a part in this process. As mentioned earlier, decision-makers can make a real difference, but we must remember that revolutions also begin from the ground up. Accessibility proves no exception.

THE ROLE OF LEADERSHIP

Each member of a museum's staff plays an important role and complements the work of colleagues. That said, accessibility requires the commitment of those in a position of leadership, alongside the availability of resources and the involvement of all staff. Due to their central role, it is important to analyze leaders and their ability to articulate and promote effective action to reach specific goals. These outcomes can be measured with qualitative data, but economic and financial metrics also need to inform the conversation.

It is interesting to note, however, that in recent years museum leadership has increasingly been involved and even rewarded for assuming a proactive focus on inclusiveness. One example is the John Cotton Dana Award for Leadership, an award established by the American Alliance of Museums in 1991 to recognize efforts of individuals (outside the field of museum education) whose work supports public and community engagement.[1] John Cotton Dana is still known for his commitment and contribution to this area. He founded the Newark Museum in New Jersey in 1909 and proposed a particularly insightful definition of museums: "A good museum attracts, entertains, arouses curiosity, leads to questioning and thus promotes learning. [. . .] The Museum can help people only if they use it; they will use it only if they know about it and only if attention is given to the interpretation of its possessions in terms they, the people, will understand."[2] According to Cotton Dana, museums' *raison d'etre* is community service.

The current debate around the role of leadership largely insists on two key aspects: Leaders need to define an inclusive model, and they must question certain responsibilities assigned to single individuals. Cultivating inclusive leadership means fostering an approach guided by listening; it is both respectful of differences and authoritative. *Harvard Business Review* recently studied a sample of 4,100 employees (outside the museum context) and concluded that an inclusive leader should demonstrate visible commitment, humility, awareness of prejudices, curiosity about others, cultural intelligence, and effective collaboration skills.[3] Such leaders are, therefore, people with a natural inclination to create a deeply collaborative environment within their institution. They insist on staff diversity and listen to their team's needs. This profile easily applies to figures required of an accessible museum.

These characteristics, however, are often the product of personal skills and attitudes and present a critical limit to museum accessibility. They force us to recognize that inclusion depends largely on a single person, regardless of whether or not they have a disability. We know that good leaders open up a dialogue with the public and promote greater access, but what happens when leaders lack this aptitude? What happens when a talented and empathetic leader leaves their role? Can we really afford to entrust such a huge responsibility to a single individual?

"Our Museum" takes a hard look at shared leadership.[4] This online platform provides a range of resources designed to illustrate the steps for building a community engagement–oriented development process. This research suggests the importance of redefining organizational and leadership management models based on concrete experiments funded by the Paul Hamlyn Foundation and carried out at several UK museums. Leadership as a participatory practice is presented as the most incisive way to develop museums that are open and capable of dealing with different perspectives.

The topic raises many questions that have yet to be resolved. What counts most is the willingness to change, and change requires, among other things, training. In our case, it is important to remember that even when accessibility training is provided by an outside organization, it is best to include people in positions of leadership. Different experiences have shown that the museums most capable of developing deep attention to access are those whose managers have made themselves personally available to do so. Leaders, including those at the head of organizations with strong hierarchical structures, need to participate in workshops often aimed at other staff members. When leaders train alongside other museum staff members, they communicate their commitment to unite their institutions, learning together and working to achieve common goals.

Establishing Your Process

ORGANIZATIONAL COMPOSITION

The first step when planning a transformation of any kind is to consider scale and method. We must first understand whether the change will involve the entire institution and whether it will be a more limited process change or also, as is more likely to be imagined, a gradual process. These issues will be explored in greater depth in chapter 10.

Rethinking the organizational makeup often implies a partial reconsideration of the organization chart. In more rigid, hierarchical models it becomes especially important to look at the degree of separation between the museum and the public. Specific procedures help promote new ways of working and encourage interdisciplinary approaches. In years past, the De Young Museum in San Francisco began planning every new exhibition in collaboration with the accessibility coordinator, whose role was to advocate for the needs of people with disabilities.[5] This working style involves step-by-step procedures, a degree of experimentation, and the support of a management team.

Organizational changes are often the most difficult to implement, but they also produce some of the most effective results. They do, however, require close attention to roles. Sara Horton, an expert accessibility consultant, has frequently stepped in as an agent of change. Her work reminds us how fundamental it is to understand that people within an organization have the responsibility or the authority to make decisions.[6] The next step involves helping the people "involved in making decisions that affect accessibility . . . to understand their role and responsibilities, and to appreciate how their decisions affect the ability of others to meet their responsibilities."[7] Another key requirement, common to all decision-making, is that the responsibility of the person leading the project must be coupled with the authority to ensure that colleagues do not need to be convinced of the importance of accessibility, but that they perceive it as a nonnegotiable process.

ACTION PLAN

The process of turning our goals into reality means using real data to draw up a checklist that will make up the stepping-stones to actuate the plan. The action plan is, therefore, a document that maps a strategy and supports the team in its work. It also helps team members to meet set deadlines and objectives. The most significant task is to define the strategy to be implemented based on established objectives. The next phase is planning specific steps and actions. Our checklists are vital tools in this process, not least because enumerating the steps entails defining priorities, timescales, and people's roles.

The action plan must be monitored carefully, but it needs to remain flexible, as it is subject to additions and variations. Given that there is a degree of risk involved in any project, early planning should take contingencies and foreseeable difficulties into account, as well as alternative solutions. A well-crafted action plan must include:

- SMART descriptions of objectives;
- Tasks and steps needed to achieve each objective;
- Specific people involved in each step;
- Deadlines and dates for monitoring and assessment;
- Any resources needed for the tasks;
- Obstacles and aids.

Drawing up an action plan may appear daunting, but it is an incredibly helpful tool in that it reveals the feasibility of the process. It has the added benefit of reassuring leadership and staff since it chunks up large tasks into small, manageable actions.

THE TRAINING

This training session seeks to outline the improving museum accessibility through a process that moves from the initial objectives up through the final evaluation. It aims to assist participants to understand both theoretical aspects of the discipline and the subject's practical application of the subject. Concrete examples help us understand whether our choices are viable, starting from a specific plan of action.

Specialized courses often fall short when it comes to illustrating feasibility, as they offer insufficient support for planning strategies. This part of a training session examines a long list of steps and sets examples all at once. When preparing your presentation, it may be helpful to break up the information with a few activities, varying the pace and encouraging participants to rework the content within a personal context. Here are sample objectives and a suggested agenda to plan your training session.

Workshop Objectives

1. Focus on the value of accessibility within systems and processes
2. Understand the most complex and challenging steps
3. Reexamine one's own role within an organization

Agenda

- Introduction and agenda
- Icebreaker
- Presentation punctuated with short activities (you can choose from the suggestions below)
- Final debriefing

Running the Workshop

Icebreaker: A postcard from the future

This is a classic exercise that asks pairs to reflect upon the future, working with a blank postcard. On one side, the participants will draw their hopes for the museum in five years' time. On the back, they will write a short message, congratulating themselves (in the present tense) on what they have accomplished as a museum while including feedback from various stakeholders. The vision for the future should be ambitious, yet realistic. Once the allotted time has elapsed, the participants will take turns sharing a few words about their work aloud, thoughts that may be written down or recorded otherwise.

- Materials: white postcards, writing utensils, and sticky tape
- Preparation: supply materials

Activity: Making order

This activity involves organizing the various steps involved in the planning and implementation process. Each group, consisting of no more than three participants, is assigned a set of cards featuring the stages of a hypothetical plan. The cards should be put in order, without forgetting that while the sequence does not always unfold in a linear fashion, some things need to take place before others. The participants can use the blank cards provided to write any additional steps that they consider essential. This exercise can be a useful starting point to facilitate an in-depth discussion about the more challenging phases. It also helps explore the reasons for prioritizing certain steps over others.

- Materials: cards with stages of a hypothetical plan, blank cards, writing utensils
- Preparation: to carry out the activity, you need to make at least twenty cards (plus some blank ones). The cards should be no less than 8 x 8 inches in size and printed on thick paper. Participants will write out the different process steps involved in an ideal accessibility-oriented path, such as "involvement of external allies," "evaluation," and "internal communication diffusion."

Activity: Pre-mortem

This activity is useful for identifying risks and possible failures, and, ideally, ways to prevent them from occurring. It is generally thought that lessons can be learned from the various successes and failures to emerge at the end of a process, whereas it would be more useful to try to foresee potential stumbling blocks at the outset. After introducing the design process aimed at accessibility, we ask each participant, "What will go wrong?" or, to raise the stakes, "How will this end in disaster?". Each person chimes in, and the concerns raised can be summarized on a board and shared verbally. The list of concerns and risks will help the group focus more closely on the action that needs to be taken first.

- Materials: flipboard and writing utensils
- Preparation: supply materials

Activity: Action plan

Defining an action plan can be a useful exercise, whether you are using real data and objectives or creating a hypothetical example for training purposes. The key is to start with smart goals: These should be written on large cards and read out loud, one at a time. Once the objectives have been shared, participants will be provided with a set of contextual details (possibly invented) and will use a template to reflect on each objective and the action that needs to be implemented to achieve them. The tasks will then be placed in chronological order and assigned to someone, along with a deadline. Later, ask the participants to identify any obstacles, problems, and solutions that might arise in the pursuit of each objective and schedule occasions to check, monitor, and review each step. To close the activity, debrief and discuss the potential of this tool.

- Materials: cards, sheets of paper
- Preparation: define the objectives and write them out on cards, making sure they are concise and highly legible. Prepare a template that enables participants to think through the tasks, starting from the individual objectives, and have a white sheet on hand for writing out the final action plan. The same template should also be available in digital form for those who prefer to complete the document using their own device.

FINAL THOUGHTS

Accessibility, like all projects, appeals to a core cognitive principle: If we observe an object or phenomenon from a macroscopic perspective, we can understand its specificities more fully. This awareness can help institutions and individual staff members when we find ourselves in unsatisfactory situations and wish to give shape to a preferable one. Accessibility harbors the desire to understand the existing world while participating in the creation of new, possible worlds. This journey is being undertaken one step at a time. It begins with a solid analysis and understanding of the point of departure.

NOTES

1. "John Cotton Dana Award for Leadership," American Alliance of Museums, accessed May 3, 2021, www.aam-us.org/programs/awards-competitions/john-cotton-dana-award-for-leadership.

2. John Cotton Dana, *The New Museum* (Woodstock, VT: Elm Tree Press, 1917).
3. Juliet Bourke and Andrea Titus, "Why Inclusive Leaders Are Good for Organizations, and How to Become One," *Harvard Business Review*, March 29, 2019, accessed April 12, 2021, https://hbr.org/2019/03/why-inclusive-leaders-are-good-for-organiza tions-and-how-to-become-one.
4. "Our Museum: Communities and Museums as Active Partners," Paul Hamlyn Foundation, accessed April 29, 2021, http://ourmuseum.org.uk.
5. Rebecca Granados, former accessibility coordinator, De Young Museum, interview by author, San Francisco, CA, August 14, 2014.
6. Sarah Horton, "Digital Accessibility and Disability Inclusion," *Sarah Horton Design* (blog), August 10, 2014, accessed April 29, 2021, https://sarahhortondesign .com/2014/08/10/organizations-accessibility-and-change.
7. Ibid.

8

Mapping Barriers and Self-Assessing Accessibility

There are many barriers that restrict people's museum experience: a label written in academic jargon, a step to access a room, a ticket that costs too much, an exhibition that only appeals to a visitor's sense of sight, a museum attendant who is unaware of how to relate to someone with an intellectual disability. Mapping such barriers accurately is crucial. The first step is to identify and understand all the existing obstacles and, before proceeding, to define priorities and strategies for their removal.

Barriers exist in every context, but they are not always easy to spot. These obstacles impact the museum experience in a myriad of ways. For example, they "can block us, slow us down, divert us from our goals, cause fatigue, limit our opportunities, or restrict our ability to express ourselves"[1] and likewise weaken the quality of the visit and limit opportunities to access content. These barriers can be material or immaterial; in both cases, they limit participation by making people feel uninvolved, inadequate, or lacking in the basic knowledge required to access museum content. It is useful to remember that a barrier is any obstacle that a visitor may encounter during their experience and that prevents them from gaining full access to a place, content, or service. Some, such as a text written in six-point font, are universal, but more often, barriers must be understood in relation to those who encounter them and whose perception will be keener or less intense according to their own needs. While a staircase may be a challenge for some, it can prove completely inaccessible to others. In other words, barriers are not absolute, but relative.

As mentioned earlier, a combination of factors renders a site inaccessible, and these agents can be highly subjective and hard to identify. What is useful to remember is the distinction between the disempowering effects of some barriers compared with others, and, most importantly, the possibility of anticipating potential difficulties in advance. For instance, a text's content and its layout make or break communication. To ensure that a museum is truly accessible, it is essential to carry out a thorough investigation of all factors that might contribute to the accessibility of an experience. All the while, it is important to consider a range of profoundly different needs and prioritize the removal of the most disabling barriers. These are often the obstacles encountered by people with sensory, cognitive, and motor disabilities.

Since obstacles are relative, our comprehension of them must also take personal motivation into account. If someone feels strongly motivated to understand a caption, they are more likely to reread it several times, even if the content is challenging. On the other hand, if they sense no urgent drive to grasp the content, they will quickly abandon any attempt to make out its meaning. Others still may find it impossible to read, despite their interest and motivation. In short, museums need to bear in mind the many variables at play.

HOW TO ANALYZE BARRIERS?

Barriers can be categorized according to various criteria. This process greatly assists us in understanding their complexities and, more importantly, their potential impact on target audiences. Jocelyn Dodd, Richard Sandell, and Alison Coles offer a useful outline that brings into focus the major barriers that museums present, including a classification of barrier types and relevant questions.[2] The following list summarizes their observations with the addition of certain issues raised in digital contexts:

- Economic: Is the admission fee accessible to people with low incomes?
- Cultural: Do the exhibitions, collections, and activities reflect the interests of the public?
- Physical: Is the museum physically accessible?
- Sensory: Are exhibits, activities, and events accessible to people with sensory disabilities?
- Technological: Does the use of technology facilitate public access?
- Linguistic: Do visitors understand the language in use?
- Intellectual: Do exhibitions exclude people with limited prior knowledge about artists and collections? Can people with cognitive disabilities access the offerings in partial autonomy?
- Emotional: Is the museum a welcoming place? Does the staff have training and an attitude of openness to diversity? Is the communication style inclusive?
- Participatory: Does the museum consult potential new audiences and take visitors' suggestions into account? Does the museum offer a representation of the audiences it would like to include?
- Elucidative: Does the communication strategy effectively reach and engage with new and regular audiences?
- Digital: Do digital tools facilitate access to contents, to information, and to the venue?

These different types of barriers need to be understood within the museum system and their presence mapped in order to locate them and evaluate their distribution. The barriers that we perceive on-site may be present at all phases and areas relating to the visitors' experience, including the website, parking, reception, informational materials provided, and the visits' very organization. It is, therefore, essential to remember the systemic nature of these barriers and their potential to pervade every aspect of the experience; barriers risk severely diminishing the quality of a visit or could even render it impossible.

Moreover, this investigation involves many areas, which include direct interactions with visitors. Since barriers are highly complex, the following pages will offer a mere glimpse at those present at entrances, in exhibition spaces, and in captions, as well as those associated with a lack of staff training, inaccessible information, and certain educational activities. This brief survey does not intend to be exhaustive; it aims at exposing the most common obstacles to readers who may be new to the topic or who are grappling with how to remove barriers for the first time.

The text has thus far focused on "direct" barriers, since they have a direct impact on the public and can be easily identified through checklists. We must add another series of barriers that, due to their structural nature, often call for more complex interventions. These may involve policy issues or missing consultation with stakeholders, aspects explored further in the next chapter.

Entrance Hall

Entrance halls have recently taken on new significance. Once seen as a secondary, they are now attracting renewed interest and becoming an important space with their own identity, considered suitable for displaying works or experimental projects. Their symbolic value is particularly significant for their ability to signal the museum's capacity to welcome visitors and guarantee friendly access. For this reason, it is believed that the entrance hall should not only be as barrier-free as possible, but it should also convey an idea of the kind of facilities available.

These suggestions are far from definitive, but they can help point museums in the right direction. Certain barriers are architectural in nature and are linked more specifically to the way visitors cross thresholds (for example, steps or a door that is too heavy to push) or to the height of furniture. To bolster visitors' autonomy, a panel that clearly explains existing facilities can prevent the creation of other potential barriers, especially for people who prefer not to make their needs explicit, like visitors with an invisible disability. This sort of panel should list all the facilities available to make visits more accessible, specifying locations of services like assistive listening systems, wheelchairs, baby carriers, noise-canceling headphones, mediation toolkits, or printed information in alternative formats: and, possibly, in multiple languages the same information that should be provided online. It is important to have an ample quantity of maps available—be they tactile, audio, or simplified—since they help visitors visualize paths in their entirety. The spread of the pandemic has made tactile aids less desirable, but other tools and personal device apps can help achieve these same goals. Another important part of the entrance is the area designated as a ticket office, which can be optimized by making sure it is clearly visible from the entrance and assessing visitors' experiences as they stand in line. This process alone can be disabling, especially when there are no seats available in the vicinity.

Exhibition Space

Complex by nature, exhibition spaces are central to the museum experience and, for this very reason, may present the most barriers for visitors. Generally speaking, barriers that exist in relation to an exhibition route might include the height at which objects are displayed, corridors' widths, slippery floors, poorly visible paths, as well as weak color contrasts between the floor, ceiling, and walls. Very long routes can pose an obstacle in terms of orientation or offer a nonlinear experience resulting in a poor grasp of the exhibition's overall development. Additional barriers include small spaces that force people into uncomfortable situations, or overcrowded museums or pathways that do not facilitate visitor flow. These issues are further compounded by absent or poorly positioned seating, videos that are inaccessible for deaf people or translated into sign language without subtitles, and pieces displayed in cases that exclude some visitors from seeing the contained objects. Another significant limitation is posed by the lack of permanent tactile and interactive opportunities, as well as footpaths or beacons that can accompany blind or visually impaired visitors. Along the itinerary, other barriers require further attention to include features like lighting, wayfinding, signage, and captions. Museum rooms that are all identical, lacking in accessible interpretative solutions, pose additional obstacles that are often underestimated.

Captions

Captions can be glaringly limited in their readability and comprehensibility, not to mention the lack of access to content. The degree of visibility is important to keep in mind, along with the captions' position in a given space or a problematic interpretative angle. Yet they have the power to guide visitors progressively through complex content when museums adopt a linear approach to captioning. This said, a detailed plan for caption contents cannot guarantee that they will be read. As mentioned earlier, Stephen Bitgood lays out a number of empirical factors that influence visitors when deciding whether or not to read captions. Most of these reasons relate to accessibility: text length; position (in terms of height and proximity to the object on display); font size and type; text density; lack of contrast to the background; content that sounds highly technical, is boring, or contains errors in grammar and syntax; methodological reading traces (such as questions); movement; multisensory input; colors; manipulative stimuli; images, diagrams; infographics; typography; ambiguous deciphering; and caption size. Clearly, caption accessibility can be developed on a variety of overlapping levels by implementing a process through which different authors concurrently appeal to sensory and physical, intellectual, cultural, and linguistic accessibility. As per comprehensibility, it is always a question of whether the content is equally comprehensible to people of different cultural or geographical origins. It is also important to ask whether the traditional order of information might demotivate certain visitors, as is the case for those captions that open with long historical references before discussing the present. With reference to content, it is also important to diversify approaches, offering answers to different, interdisciplinary questions as there are those who seek to understand phenomena as well as those who wonder about their causes or future developments.

Positioning a caption appropriately favors its readability, so solutions should start by considering contextual factors such as lighting and the order in which information is presented. Color contrast, typeface and type, and the use of nonreflective surfaces play important roles in visitor experience. By its very nature, it is important to remember that captioning is not accessible for everyone. For example, braille texts allow blind people to read captions, but numerous studies indicate it is more effective to provide minimal texts due to the limited mobility experienced by blind people, particularly when navigating unfamiliar places. Furthermore, knowledge of this writing system is more limited than often believed. User experience expresses a growing preference for more effective tools, like audio solutions made available through personal devices and other mobile technology. Obviously, the use of personal devices makes additional needs evident, such as not consuming all the memory and being able to easily charge the battery.

Lack of Staff Training

Insufficient staff training constitutes another significant barrier, for example, when a reception staff is unable to help visitors, facilitate their experience, or provide accurate information about the museum's accessibility. The ability to relate appropriately to different people is a vital skill that can be acquired with the right training. For example, it is about not making people feel inadequate if they do not know the content of the museum or if they speak aloud, but also about knowing that communication with a deaf person can be significantly aided by having a pen handy, especially while wearing a nontransparent facemask. Trained staff can usually handle unexpected situations with greater flexibility, a key requirement especially when engaging with people who have cognitive disabilities.

Moreover, the staff's attitude is a crucial component to help people feel at ease from the very beginning of their visit. It is best for staff to avoid coming across as intrusive or heavy-handed, even with the best intentions. It used to be common for well-intentioned museum volunteers to pick people up in wheelchairs and then carry them across entrance steps. Despite the goodwill, this approach is unacceptable from a safety standpoint, but especially because it can undermine personal dignity.

Staff training is essential for sharing more than information about certain kinds of visitors, but also to introduce them to visitor studies. In the best-case scenario, staff and volunteers can make a decisive contribution to visitor experiences by monitoring how the public behaves in and around museums, as well as their potential barriers.

Lack of Accessible Information

Accessible web design featured earlier in the book, but how can we provide accessible information in museums themselves? On the ground, information is often noticeably thin and lacks the diversity that would make it accessible to different people. Like pathways themselves, information often fails to meet minimal guidelines for achieving effective or even basic communication. Moreover, communication ought to be understood in a broad and unstructured way. It does not occur only through text printed on paper but can take on many formats: the use of audio-video materials or text and images that are printed or posted online. Today, information comes across as increasingly accessible thanks to different media channels like apps, electronic documents, and online resources.

In the case of brochures and paper-based information, the most widespread barriers may be dictated by the material itself. For instance, glossy and reflective surfaces, as well as other elements, can hamper readability and comprehensibility. In addition, brochures often come in just one format, without large print or more accessible alternatives, and this makes it impossible for some to access them. It is helpful to make these materials available online, enabling people to use them through assistive devices or other tools.

On a linguistic front, texts can engage the largest possible number of visitors when they cater to "the most common of common denominators." For one, it is also important to keep in mind that long texts might discourage most visitors. In fact, experts advise against the use of overly complex sentences to avoid frustrating visitors, regardless of their language and comprehension skills. Careful to avoid bland content, museums need to provide simple, but not simplistic communication.

A final consideration relates to the way museums give directions and inform visitors about the premise's accessibility. This information is seldom shared or is often limited to entrances that cater to specific motor needs. It is helpful to describe the intrinsic accessibility of the whole building, as well as that of the experiences on offer.

Educational Activities

We are accustomed to thinking that educational activities are always accessible, and above all, that they represent solutions and are without any barriers. Whether they are aimed at adults, children, or those with specific needs, these activities can be equally risky in terms of the barriers. As in all contexts, the first obstacle is posed by the lack of a positive climate, meaning one that favors learning and co-involvement. In guided tours, for example, we often fail to develop solutions that allow people with different visual and auditory abilities to access content. Or we take for granted certain backgrounds in knowledge. These barriers emerge whenever the relationship leaves little room for listening to the recipients' needs.

Numerous barriers can emerge when the group is composed of a class. Museum environments can overload visitors with stimuli. It is helpful to propose diversified activities and to bear in mind the needs of individuals within a group. These are just a few examples that can make an educational program more effective and accessible for everyone involved.

MAPPING BARRIERS

If we are to consider accessibility as a process, then the first step in its development entails an investigation into an organization's barriers and a full elaboration of these findings. Without a rigorous assessment of existing obstacles, it is difficult for museums to remove barriers in a sequential and appropriate manner. By virtue of limited resources, however, many environments feel they have little choice. Provided that legal requirements have already been fulfilled, most museums opt to focus on removing certain barriers over others, largely based on contingent factors like demand from a particular type of user, complaints about specific barriers, or model experiences that are relatively easy to replicate. These responses help illustrate that an institution will inevitably misunderstand its priorities if it does not appeal to an overarching plan that enumerates inherent complexities and helps guide in-house choices.

Mapping out barriers is a fundamental step with several benefits. Firstly, this process allows us to understand which barriers can be contained without much effort. This is an opportunity for institutions to rethink the complexity of a visitor's experience from the user's point of view. Moreover, when recipients are involved in the mapping experience, museums develop stronger and more informed relationships with them.

A myriad of strategies can be employed, but a multiple-step approach tends to be most effective. To begin with, there are three possible degrees of people's involvement in the process: staff who are directly implicated, the inclusion of the initial group and all other staff, and lastly involving experts and users with different needs to verify the effectiveness of given actions. The use of the various tools required for this process and in training will be addressed shortly, while the involvement of people from outside the museum will be explored further in the next chapter.

If proceeding this way proves operationally unmanageable, the priority should be to self-assess barriers, potentially through a simplified method of analysis. It is easier to plan this in small- or medium-sized organizations, so the size of the museum can be a discriminating factor. It is important to accompany this process with relevant training across the board to increase the staff's awareness of the issues at play. Provided that there are adequate financial resources, another alternative can be to outsource the process. External professionals can carry out a structured audit to assess and test singularly the functionality of different services, places, and tools.

As mentioned in chapter 7, taking a visitor-oriented perspective means retracing the user's visitor experience in a linear fashion. This kind of survey can focus on a single aspect (like the website or captions), or more commonly, it examines existing barriers along the visitor's route. It is important to include alternative paths used by people with reduced mobility in this analysis. We will later see that it is sometimes necessary to distinguish between a process to initiate during training, and the actual mapping, which can prove complex and require several days (or even months), depending on the size of the museum or the area under investigation.

When attempting to gain a full understanding of existing or potential barriers, some institutions invite their planners and colleagues to a simulation whereby they embark on a museum visit with their eyes closed or moving through the space in a wheelchair. This method is often memorable to many and can be helpful in raising awareness about barriers, but it can also be considered questionable, as it does not truly put the person in a position to comprehend needs and skills. In fact, this exercise risks merely mimicking a condition of disability. This type of *mise-en-scène* can even lead to an overperception of barriers, given that those experiencing this condition have no experience in managing it and therefore have a skewed impression of an obstacle's effects. By involving stakeholders directly or by creating dedicated programs, museums can avoid these pitfalls and truly build empathetic relationships with people and their diverse needs.

A variety of tools and testing methods can be sourced from user-experience design, the field that regularly employs a wide range of techniques to measure the efficacy of a product, place, or service. For example, the use of personas in the investigation process can help the planning team shift perspective. Since it is challenging to try to pinpoint needs that are different from our own, this tool defines user archetypes and can be extremely effective in identifying other people's possible motivations, expectations, and barriers. To avoid promoting stereotypes, it is important is to establish a number of multi-faceted user profiles that cover a considerable range of perspectives. For Alan Cooper, a pioneer in this technique, the value of this exercise derives from the observation that "The most obvious approach—to find the actual user and ask him—doesn't work for a number of reasons, but the main one is that merely being the victim of a particular problem doesn't automatically bestow on one the power to see a solution."[3]

Visitor journeys can prove useful in similar ways but should be used after exploring how personas interact with barriers. This complementary technique articulates the story behind the actors and their actions and considers the feelings and perceptions that can emerge before a product or space at a given time. The premise of this experience model is to put oneself in other people's shoes as they experience a sequence of events. It can be used to document or improve existing activities and to prototype new ones. Real data from visitor research can be plugged into visitor journeys while tracking the experience of different individuals. Furthermore, this technique provides a useful resource for a team of people who are problem-solving collectively.

One of the most important outcomes of this process is a series of checklists that provide an exhaustive inventory of any barriers that constitute objective limitations. These specifications can be tied to the museum space, but they could also apply to a website, or to a single deliverable instrument or project that needs to be appraised. In the English-speaking world, the best-known lists for spatial and communication analysis were developed by the Smithsonian Institute and the Canadian Museum for Human Rights in Winnipeg.[4] The Canadian example is more up-to-date and easier to consult, but both provide frameworks for identifying direct barriers and are readily available online. The sequential use of these tools, from personas to checklists, allows investigators to perceive existing barriers more clearly by engaging their intuition and empathy and enhancing this work with a precise set of references.

THE TRAINING

The proposed workshop helps one understand and investigate barriers. It is intended to be part of a broader process, but, for some colleagues, it can constitute an isolated encounter. For example, this training exercise can involve staff from other areas and generally broaden institutional awareness of present obstacles. But when effectively carried out, this kind of activity can also feed into concrete investigations and provide useful material for a more structured audit. This training session is appropriate both for students and museum professionals and can be carried out in one's own museum context or in an external setting on the condition that participants have the necessary material at their disposal. On its own, however, it does not constitute an exhaustive solution for barrier removal.

If conducted in a museum space other than the one in which a participant already works, it is especially important to debrief the types of barriers, but also to explore the reasons they may be there in the first place. While the absence of accessible approaches is often due to a lack of knowledge or attention, there can, in fact, be contingent limitations that have prevented their implementation. A full understanding of a barrier's context and its reasons for existing can help shift the conversation away from superficial solutions and prevent confrontational exchanges. Mindful of each institution's specific history, it is especially important to withhold judgment regarding the preexistence of barriers. When partnering with other museums, workshops like this one should emphasize mutual transformation and learning.

To be as effective and accessible as possible, trainers ought to remember to take a dynamic approach, engaging their audience by asking questions and leaving room for personal interpretation. They should present content in a linear fashion and introduce essentials, such as the definition of a barrier, their various natures, their dissemination throughout the museum system, and ways to identify them. It is important to include examples from beyond the museum context. Adequate preparation also makes a difference, and some activities require tools to be gathered in advance, as indicated below.

Workshop Objectives

1. Introduce the concept of barriers and solicit an analytical understanding of them;
2. Promote understanding of the diversity of needs;
3. Provide tools and solutions to map barriers present in a given context, product, or service.

The Agenda

- Introduction and agenda
- Icebreaker
- Presentation
- Activity
- Final debrief

Running the Workshop

Icebreaker

Make a series of cards depicting the different barriers that people might encounter in their daily lives, but that are difficult to spot. For example, everyone has dealt with narrow turnstiles in the subway or illegibly printed ingredients on a food label. To get your point across, it can be useful to use clever or surreal images like *The Imaginary Museum* (1987), a well-known artwork by Hans Hollein that depicts a museum gallery with giant captions for tiny artworks.

At the beginning of the activity, all the images should be visually described by the facilitator. There are various prompts to be used in various ways:

- Each person chooses a card depicting a barrier they have encountered personally, and they introduce themselves through this experience.
- Each person chooses a card depicting a barrier that they tend to underestimate and shares the reasons for this with the group.
- The group must find a criterion for putting these barriers in order and then work together to decide an appropriate sequence.

There should be more cards than participants, and all images used must be well contrasted, printed in color, on thick paper that measures at least 8 x 8 inches. The key is to keep up the activity's pace to ensure that it stays dynamic and to close with a debrief.

Activity: From personas to guidelines

This activity can be very effective and can profoundly empower its participants. It unfolds in three stages and includes the use of both personas and the guidelines, materials prepared in advance with the aid of the instructions in the section entitled "Preparation." Following the Principle of Progressive Disclosure, each step should be introduced one at a time to clarify from the outset that the task is divided into different chunks. It is also useful to mention that the activity will conclude with a collective review of the experience. One should mind the steps and keep time to ensure the activity's success.

The first step is a free exploration to identify the barriers that could be related to an exhibition space, to communication materials, or to a website, depending on the area of observation chosen. This action should be carried out individually with no specific prompts provided other than the information shared during the presentation. For the sake of time (no more than twenty-five minutes), it is advisable to avoid exploring too large a space and to opt instead for a section of the museum, unless the trainer adjusts the workshop's timing to examine a more complex space. It may be fitting to use the entrance hall and one or two rooms as a case study or to compare two museum websites or a small set of brochures. In any case, participants should explore this place or these materials independently to give everyone a chance to put their skills to the test. When the set time has elapsed, the group reconvenes, and the participants are assigned a new task. There will be time to give feedback later.

In the second phase, the participants split off into groups with their own assignment: Each one reads about a set of personas and goes on to conduct a second analysis. This time, however, they need to consider new needs. Once they receive the persona cards, the groups organize themselves without making any written notes; they discuss all the new barriers they meet among themselves.

The groups get a heads-up five minutes before the time expires, and once the allotted time has elapsed, they move on to a third and final phase. During this step, participants remain in the same groups and are given a simplified version of a checklist to help them conduct a more precise analysis of the elements they had only guessed at in the previous phase. At the end of the allotted time (no less than twenty-five minutes), all groups are asked to return to the plenary session to debrief together. This setting provides everyone with the opportunity to discuss not only the barriers they identified, but also the invisibility of certain barriers, the usefulness of different tools, and what they have learned from this activity.

Like most of those proposed in this book, this workshop can also be conducted online. In this context, it could be interesting to employ personas and then to survey at least the most visible obstacles present, for example, on a museum website. Whether or not this exercise is applied to the specificities of a physical location, it conveys a valuable method that widens the focus beyond a limited set of contents.

- Materials: paper of different thicknesses, textures, and colors, and/or cards measuring 8 x 8 inches, scissors, markers, flipchart
- Preparation: consisting of two parts: (1) making personas and (2) defining checklists

Making personas

Creating effective personas requires some practice, but they can ultimately prove extremely effective. For this workshop, you will need a minimum of six and no more than eight different profiles, which are to be printed on thick paper to create a series of cards, if possible, of a different shape and paper texture than those used for the icebreaker. These personas can be also created in audio format and/or shared online. In order to keep the workshop moving at a timely pace, the use of relatively short texts is recommended. These should clearly convey the needs in question so that even a participant who is new to the subject can easily engage in the workshop. So if someone does not know the specific requirements of a person who has suffered a stroke, for example, the participant should have no trouble taking part in the workshop.

Personas can be developed on the basis of qualitative and quantitative data, or they can be fictitious characters constructed from a designer's experience. In the latter case, the trainer will need to take care to create engaging but purely indicative profiles that steer clear of stereotypes. This is why these figures are given interests, passions, and characteristics that veer away from clichés, as well as aspects related to race, ethnicity, gender, age, sexual orientation, personality, professional identities, and so on, to make their identities complex and multifaceted.

When looking at the descriptions as a whole, participants need to find themselves face-to-face with a hypothetical group that represents as many needs as possible. Ultimately, the workshop asks them to put themselves in the shoes of people with different needs from one another and from themselves.

Defining checklists

Tailored checklists are vital tools for facilitating the workshop's logistics and timing. They should be detailed but not too long, and therefore not the final ones to be used in real mapping. When checking the barriers present in a brochure, for instance, the list could consist of about twenty points divided into different issue areas, as seen in the example below:

Readability

- Is there sharp color contrast between text and background?
- Is the font size large enough (at least 12 points)?
- Are there paragraph headings?
- Is the information in the correct, progressive order?
- Does the most important info stand out (for example, in bold)?
- Are there relatively short blocks of text and bulleted lists that make reading easier?
- Is the text all left-aligned and never justified?
- Are there images beneath the text that do not allow it to be read correctly?
- Contrast: Is there a clear contrast between colors? Are there any graphics or images beneath the text that risk making it unreadable?
- Is the text free from underlined or italicized words that make it difficult to read?
- Is the brochure material opaque, thick, or nonreflective?
- Is there sufficient spacing in the text?

Understandability

- Is information about the program, products, and services written in easy-to-read language with active sentences and no subordinate clauses?
- Is the main content of the text made explicit in a clear, concise, and straightforward introductory text?
- Are images sufficiently visible, relevant, and understandable?
- Are words kept to a minimum, and, if so, are they explained?

Information for accessibility

- Is there information for people with specific needs?
- Is the language used inclusive and person-centered?
- Is the information available in multiple languages?

Alternative formats

- Are brochures available in extra-large format?
- Is the same information available on the website or via an app?
- Is the text also available in audio format?

When developing this tool, it is important to adhere to the outlined guidelines by highlighting key aspects on which you want your participants to focus. More detailed checklists can, of course, be used, but one would have to recalibrate timing to dedicate several days to the mapping alone.

FINAL THOUGHTS

As stated thus far, mapping barriers is a fundamental step in increasing accessibility: to be fully aware of existing limitations, to be able to share them with visitors and, above all, to know which ones can be removed before others. While the practical benefits may seem obvious, it is equally important to cultivate a new mindset that insists on a method that begins with adequate analysis and goes on to propose new solutions and designs; this approach proves useful across the board, from curatorship to management to everyday life. It also allows staff to come to grips with the difficulties that museums can generate and brings about an awareness that empowers them to help realize more effective changes.

NOTES

1. Edward Steinfeld and Jordana L. Maisel, *Universal Design: Creating Inclusive Environments* (Hoboken, NJ: Wiley, 2012).
2. Jocelyn Dodd, Richard Sandell, and Alison Coles, *Building Bridges: Guidance for Museums Galleries on Developing Audiences* (London: Museums and Galleries Commission, 1998).
3. Jenn Visocky O'Grady and Ken Visocky O'Grady, *A Designer's Research Manual*, 2nd ed. (Beverly, MA: Rockport, 2017), 90.
4. Smithsonian Institute, "Smithsonian Guidelines for Accessible Exhibition Design," revised March 2011, accessed April 28, 2012, www.sifacilities.si.edu/sites/default/files/Files/Accessibility/accessible-exhibition-design1.pdf; Canadian Museum of Human Rights, "Inclusive and Accessible Guidelines," accessed on April 28, 2012, https://id.humanrights.ca/.

9

Co-design

FINDING YOUR ALLIES

Accessibility forges a connection between human beings. Recognizing the needs of others is not only the right thing to do, but it is essential for our mutual coexistence. In the context of an organization, this subject must be embodied in an institution's form and intentions. As such, it poses an extraordinary opportunity to redefine internal processes while establishing and reinforcing relationships with the outside world. Clearly, change can happen only when a group of people shares a set of common values and aspires to achieve the same goals. In fact, it is unreasonable to expect a single person to manage a stable, structured, and systemic process alone. As mentioned earlier, this process must be adopted endemically if it is to take full effect; a widespread application implies that people who occupy a range of different roles all embrace accessibility.

Both theory and experience show that organizational transformation, or even the adoption of a few new practices, is one of the most complex challenges an institution can face. It is difficult in terms of structure and general management. It is also challenging for those who feel they are already fulfilling their duties, like staff members who have already established a relationship with the public but whose responsibilities are not directly associated with accessibility. Understandably, these museum workers may feel overwhelmed when asked to acquire new skills as they are effectively carrying out their given tasks.

Reinforcing shared values within an organization can help different staff members become more aware of the overlap between their work and accessibility, helping ease eventual resistance to the subject. It is no coincidence that different people in an organization often perform complementary functions, without any real opportunity for exchange: Each pursues different goals, thus avoiding the risk of potential conflict as they stay "protected" by the distinct specificities of their discipline. As we will see, these situations often derive from the very structure of an organizational chart and reflect a series of apparently invisible choices that impact accessibility and every visitor's experience.

With all this in mind, it becomes evident that it is as critical as it is challenging to plan a process that fully engages diverse people and coworkers, united in their advocacy for the importance of accessibility. This kind of transformation can be promoted from the bottom up or from the top down. Starting from the direction, all staff need allies on every level, including coworkers, managers, volunteers, and stakeholders, as well as the public and communities close to the museum. This requires the kind of commitment that generates new visions and promotes partici-patory processes involving motivated people with a wealth of experience. Whether internal or external, allies must be regarded as problem-solvers in a participatory process whose outcome cannot be guaranteed. That said, this approach is poten-tially among the most effective in finding solutions, enhancing accessibility, and more.

Looking for allies means identifying people who are interested in change and available for support, starting from those who are closest. A motivated and diverse group of people can tap in to a body of skills, needs, and interests and has the capacity to solve a problem more effectively than a homogeneous group, even one made up entirely of experts. Engaging with a diverse range of allies also generates solutions to a variety of needs, making it possible to recalibrate an offering that was conventionally handed over from the top down and has remained disconnected from its final recipients and their requirements.

INTERNAL ALLIES

In order for accessibility to take on the importance it deserves within the visitor experience, museums need to stop treating it as an accessory measure that can be handled by one individual or a small group. The discipline requires someone to coordinate activities and a process, while its goals need to be pursued throughout all areas of the organization. To turn this idea into reality, we need allies like col-leagues who work in other areas and have different roles within the museum, while sharing a willingness to reassess the importance of different audiences and their far-ranging needs.

To varying degrees across the world, institutions are readying for this kind of shift. More and more organizations are choosing to assign positive value to issues around inclusion, and many actively encourage this attitude. Due to a lack of com-mitment from their leaders, some institutions have not yet managed to establish virtuous processes, while others believe minimum accessibility measures are suffi-cient. Herein, participation can make the difference.

In recent years, the conversation around internal allies has focused mainly on the need to reinforce their awareness on others' needs and, consequently, on the role of empathy. Owing to a certain rhetoric that has built up around the latter, the propensity to feel solidarity with others has not always been fully understood. We know for certain that empathy can be cultivated if it is regarded as a driving force in a process of change; it requires patience, motivation, specific requirements, and strategies. Aware that organizations need this aptitude to be solid, we cannot afford again to rely solely on the contribution of those who are spontaneously empathetic. According to Mike Murawski, author of the recent book *Museums as Agents of Change: A Guide to Becoming a Changemaker*, a new museum culture begins with those who have the ability to understand empathy and who seek out active support from leadership. This work is founded on empathy and requires both individual and organizational effort.[1]

This process can look very different depending on whether it emerges from the ground up (without initial managerial consensus) or is imposed from the top down (i.e., directed by decision-makers). The former approach is the more complex of the two and demands the support and involvement of those closest to you before extending across as many levels as possible. The advantage here is that grassroots involvement fosters a greater degree of commitment. There are small efforts that can go a long way, like helping people understand the rationale behind a new approach, sharing best practices, highlighting their feasibility, and encouraging a long-term vision. These actions help consolidate collegial support before colleagues become influencers themselves. Curators, communications managers, technology and digital managers, educators, and even management have great responsibilities in this process, and it is vital to demonstrate this agency. By adopting new procedures or even new tools, all these figures have the power to make a meaningful contribution to accessibility. Yet this journey needs to be taken one step at a time to gradually involve the whole museum; it is crucial to receive the full support of decision-makers and leadership, and ensure that those who hold positions of authority have a clear operational understanding of the benefits and impacts that only a well-structured process can generate. In slightly smaller organizations, insights and gentle pushes may even come from outside the institution. A daylong workshop or a space to share museums' experiences with similar strategies are two approaches that have generated positive results in institutions. Another option could be to invite promoters.

With a leader's support, an in-depth exploration of these issues can take on a more structured dimension. Refresher courses and training sessions—especially those that are guided and interactive—offer an ideal opportunity to share content, methods, concerns, and, most importantly, values and expertise. Professional development plays a vital role in enabling the working group to perceive the target audience differently and sheds light on prejudices and preconceptions. In addition, group work creates space for sharing reflections, points of view, and knowledge.

Effective strategies for rallying allies around inclusive measures at museums include three types of activities: *motivational* (useful for urging the need for change), *framing* (necessary for changing perceptions), and *process* (related to the process of change itself and linked to a hypothetical action plan).[2] Once internal museum staff gains greater awareness of these issues, newly trained figures should also be involved in the planning process. These steps can take place through several stages: at the outset, when defining objectives, when designing solutions, or even at the verification stage. As colleagues recognize a deliberate structure and sustained involvement in the process, they perceive more support and expertise from above, creating an effective and positive feedback system. The action plan developed in this phase can complement the initial plan proposed in chapter 7. It is important to address decision-makers' concerns and to identify potential misunderstandings about accessibility and its relevance to the whole museum.

The success of the process is contingent on numerous prerequisites, including solid support from management, the skills of those who coordinate it, a clear-cut definition of roles, and a detailed exploration of many practical examples. With regard to the aims of the change in question, these can vary greatly according to the situation, ranging from modifying organizational models, to carrying out a more detailed reflection on the organizational structure itself, to adopting new procedures, as we shall see in the next chapter.

EXTERNAL ALLIES

Museums are never islands, and in recent years they have markedly improved their ability to listen and recognize the inestimable value of connecting with different people across a number of contemporary institutions. Despite growing attention to different issues like inclusion and participation, these practices are not always effectively implemented. Participatory design requires a particular array of skills, ranging from planning to group management, facilitation, and conflict management—areas that not all museums are equipped to handle. Even where these functions are present at museums, the most frequent perception is that topics like accessibility, community, and participation constitute separate entities.

Community-oriented practice can help institutions and staff identify external allies, encouraging involvement through a wide assortment of methods and varying degrees of intensity, even where accessibility is concerned. These practices can range from seeking a simple consultation to setting up established committees that are fully engaged in the growth and development of the museum. They might also include proposals of differing levels of complexity, based on a recognition of expertise demonstrated by other institutions. On a more superficial level, we might find approaches that principally respond to the need for cognitive stimulation, as, for example, in the use of open questions or Post-its designed to engage visitors. These tools can produce useful material for consultations provided that the information gathered is subsequently processed and detailed in a report. Their scope will otherwise be limited to maintaining the attention of those present through minor interactions.

A well-conducted process can help broaden the social range of the visitor base and facilitate the inclusion of new recipients. This procedure involves them as experts and cements an institution's relationship with audiences that are already familiar with it. Although no one can guarantee success, it is important to be aware of real potential raised by certain issues like establishing a community around a museum that is yet to be built, undertaking a process of mapping barriers, or even defining new tools or prototypes for accessibility.

Developed at the Andy Warhol Museum, the project entitled *Out Loud* provides a strong case study on the benefits of this approach. It stemmed from inclusive design and aimed at ensuring the maximum autonomy for each user by considering their different perspectives.[3] For this, *Out Loud* won the Gold Muse award from the Media and Technology Committee of the American Alliance of Museums (AAM). This iOS app was designed for users of all abilities and aimed to accompany visitors through "the experience of feeling reproductions and visualizing the original artwork," with the aid of Bluetooth technology.[4]

The project's design process is especially noteworthy due to the presence of an interdepartmental project team as well as an interdisciplinary advisory team composed of experts in digital technology, museum interpretation and content, accessibility, and inclusion. In addition, the project involved people with different fields of expertise and users who gave feedback and advice. The team members report about the complexity of the user testing process, affirming that "all decisions were shaped by input from user/experts and local disability groups"[5] while testing interactive prototypes, specific components, a beta version of the app, and its accessories. The involvement of different people is more than a mere methodological choice; the output reflects the different voices and perspectives in the product's contents. Since the design phase mainly involved people with disabilities, evaluations targeted sighted visitors after the product launch to have as wide a perspective as possible. This articulated process ensured the full accessibility of the final product.

In addition to apps, exhibitions can be developed according to similar principles. Recently described as one of the topmost accessible exhibitions in the world, the Wellcome Collection's *Being Human* is a permanent exhibit designed in collaboration with the Research Centre for Museums and Galleries (RCMG) of Leicester University (UK). The two institutions adopted a participatory approach and directly involved people and experts with disabilities, who, in turn, offered their expertise regarding strategies, content development, and issues regarding representation.[6]

Another example from the National Center for Craft and Design focused on ways to decline the engagement process itself in an accessible way.[7] The Center developed a participatory design research project aimed at understanding how to cost-effectively design and curate exhibits that are intellectually accessible to visitors with visual impairments. Their work included people with visual impairments as well as elderly participants and took special care to calibrate all the supportive materials. For example, images were made in a larger format than usual, and documents adhered to the accessibility guidelines of the Royal National Institute for the Blind. The cultural institution wrote:

> visual imagery was also printed or mounted onto thin cards to aid with close up consideration. In some instances text and imagery was projected to facilitate collaborative re-designs to occur. As trust was built the sighted participants learnt to verbalize the visual imagery and explain more fully design and curatorial ideas, concepts and solutions for the blind participants. Braille documentation was not used as the blind participants did not read Braille. Lego figures and blocks were used in one workshop to explore the exhibition layout, way-finding and visitor experience. Small-scale card models of the proposed multi-sensory desks were also produced, which could be easily handled. Prototypes of touching objects were also 3D printed for evaluation and discussion.[8]

What emerges from these experiences is the importance assigned to methodology, prioritizing it alongside contents and results. An attentive method provides a myriad of meaningful learning opportunities.

Another aspect that emerges is that dividing participants into subgroups with similar needs facilitates the process, though it remains important to create opportunities for broader discussion to devise solutions that are suitable for different participants. Moreover, it is important to reflect on the stage at which you choose to involve people. This will depend on many factors, including the budget and available time—arguably the most important consideration to make—but also the ability to manage the process effectively. In an ideal world, it would be preferable to opt for long running, wide-reaching, and structured processes, but clearly this is not always feasible.

Direct experience confirms that projects involving joint planning require ample time. A prevalent misconception is to equate people with a lifetime experience with disabilities and the capacity to design accessible products and services. Having specific needs does not automatically translate into a capacity for design. People can collaborate in the assessment process by saying what works or does not thanks to skills acquired during their life experience. The design process, however, calls for professional knowledge that can consider the "big picture." Such awareness requires a designer's know-how, a skill set that most users have not mastered. If there is insufficient time, it is best to avoid sharing responsibilities and roles in the whole planning process. Parents and children offer a salient example. They are unlikely to be able to tell us how to design an activity for their kids or peers, despite having a solid understanding of what they like or dislike or can manage. It is therefore crucial to set aside time to bring knowledge, best practices, and personal experience into alignment, knowing full well that a shared design experience is always a good investment. Facilitators can help coordinate this co-design process.

This sort of interdisciplinary effort is all the more important in museum spaces where specific disciplinary and methodological issues related to the sector should always be kept in mind. One principle of participation is to ask people involved only about what they know. In this sense, participation is founded on the involvement of individuals whose knowledge has not necessarily been acquired through conventional training, but who nonetheless possess the necessary tools and experience to make a contribution. These people have been described as "alternative experts" by Sarah Smed, director of the Danish Welfare Museum, meaning that their knowledge is not traditional or disciplinary in the strictest sense, but is no less important for that, either in terms of content or competence.[9]

The Castello d'Albertis in Genoa, Italy, offers a poignant example. Located in the Ligurian capital, this historic house-museum employed co-design within a wider process dedicated to cognitive accessibility at the museum. The project involved people with intellectual disabilities, their caregivers, and experts in museum accessibility in rewriting captions in easy-to-read language. The informal group who collaborated in evaluating and rewriting texts involved the most qualified people for this particular task.[10] It is worth noting that this initiative was made possible thanks to a well-established network of local organizations.

As mentioned above, co-design methods can range from a simple consultation to a long-standing engagement. If direct contact with local associations is not already in place, it could be worth looking into issuing an open call to users with different needs who are willing to test new accessibility pathways and initiatives. On occasions like this, people are asked to behave as they typically would in given spaces, reporting back about the barriers they encounter, and contributing to the discussion through guided interviews or focus groups.

Another way to approach co-design is through the work of deep-rooted committees with rotating membership. Steering committees, for example, are working groups composed of different people (like activists, supporters, people with different needs, etc.) who can help a museum maintain an active dialogue with their community. As per accessibility, they are the first point of reference when tackling new projects, and they provide a special channel for developing relationships with different groups. This is the dynamic that emerged at the Tenement Museum in New York, for instance, where an access advisory council has been the first port of call for accessibility for some years.[11]

Lastly, there are certain considerations for museums that delegate activities relating to accessibility planning to external entities. These initiatives must respect specific design skills, but even when an activity's objectives have been defined together, oversight must reside with the museum. When delegating important responsibilities to external organizations, certain aspects of the museum experience risk being distorted. The effectiveness of these operations, therefore, requires a delicate balance of multifaceted skills from within the museum. While outside organizations can assist in making offerings more accessible, it is unadvisable to

Co-design

delegate too much. They may have specific expertise on certain topics but not regarding interpretation or representation, issues that directly involve museum experts. Delegating certain parts of accessibility planning always poses some risks and should never be regarded as a substitute for a truly participatory process.

THE CHALLENGES

Effective participation depends on the involvement of individuals who can act as spokespeople for different groups and those who are interested in and aware of their role as agents of change. Transparency is vital when it comes to sharing the purpose of this process—firstly for ethical reasons and, secondly, to avoid misunderstandings about the scope of the commitment. This topic becomes especially sensitive when a project ends abruptly, perhaps due to the interruption of funding. It is important to tend to the expectations of fragile recipients, those at risk of social exclusion who may have been led to believe there was a possibility of a long-term relationship. The question to ask ourselves is always the same: Who needs what we are doing?

When it comes to the involvement of external subjects in participatory practices, it is essential to delineate a mutually beneficial collaboration and take care not to slip into a patronizing dynamic. In the book *Museum Activism*, Bernadette Lynch reminds us that it is crucial to veer away from the rhetoric of false participation, based on the premise that the museum "wants to help" someone.[12] This motivation will result in action that can be useless if not outright harmful, generating unbalanced relationships and reinforcing existing stereotypes. As Marianella Sclavi and Laurence Susskind suggest in their work on conflict negotiation, it is wise to shift the focus from people's positions to their interests.[13] It is worthwhile to share goals, emphasize and/or restore equal value to opposing points of view, and adopt the inclusive approach, as suggested earlier.

We face many challenges that break down into a series of choices to be made by measuring risks or limitations. These might include failing to give due consideration to different positions and roles, starting participatory processes without knowing how to manage them, or inviting people to take part in a decision-making process that has no real chance of coming to fruition. Other recurring missteps are: uncertain coordination ("In the focus group, visitors say that the museum has to close: Director, what should we do?"), a failure to find participants who are truly representative ("There's no point inviting them because we know they don't care"), the solicitation of criticism and complaints ("List everything you don't like"), questions that require technical knowledge ("Let's ask visitors what anti-COVID solutions we should adopt at the museum!"), and the risk of trivializing content when participants have not been offered the necessary framework through which they can understand an object ("People suggest including the fact that they liked the artwork in the caption").

Overall, participation makes way for possibilities, but also for complexity. The traditional image of the museum as a kind of crystal gallery must be dismantled in favor of a new design culture that simultaneously welcomes multiple perspectives into a naturally difficult process. This method recognizes the importance of product *and* process. It encourages the ability to work flexibly, investing as much time as necessary and instilling a reciprocal ability to listen and suspend judgment. Above all, this process favors relationships and exchange.

THE TRAINING

This training session pivots around the topic of allies and co-design and high-lights the needs and opportunities that emerge through a shared approach to the discipline. It explores ways of broadening the adoption of accessibility practices and underlines their feasibility. Through clear and concrete examples, curatorial colleagues learn how to take a greater interest in inclusive strategies. Furthermore, it implicates the importance of ongoing training for custodians. These two, precise actions demonstrate how accessibility is a concern shared by the whole museum.

The choice of people involved in the training will naturally impact the way the workshop will unfold. If the participants are coworkers who are already aware of the needs in question, the training can broaden earlier conversations, substantiate practices, or extend to external allies. If the meeting is aimed at participants from several different museums, however, it would be more useful to allow space for an in-depth discussion that provides insight into each person's role within their own organization and help them spell out how to ignite potential change.

As always, the training session strikes a balance between theory and practice, delivering theoretical foundations first, and going on to present practical sugges-tions with concrete examples of structured planning. The organizer ought to focus on applying the method of co-design, being mindful of the trainees' modes of par-ticipation or lack thereof. In all training scenarios, it is important to leave sufficient time for discussion and a final wrap-up.

Workshop Objectives

1. Share methods and principles of participation
2. Make explicit why accessibility necessitates a shared approach
3. Facilitate a fruitful dialogue on these issues
4. Stimulate new dynamics and include the concerns of those who fear change

The Agenda

*   Introduction and agenda
*   Icebreaker
*   Presentation

- Activity
- Final debrief

Running the Workshop

Icebreaker: Deconstructing stereotypes/grouping game

For a training session dedicated to participation, an icebreaker offers an effective way of promoting empathy by highlighting similarities between different people. This particular exercise helps challenge stereotypes and takes inspiration from a commercial entitled "All that we share," which was created and broadcast by the Danish network TV2.[14] This activity works especially well with groups of twenty people or more. To begin, participants stand wherever they choose in the space. The facilitator explains how they will call several groups and ask the participants to stand either at the speaker's left or right, according to their responses to the questions posed. Those who prefer can choose to move along the wall in order not to lose their bearings, clearly defining a precise point that distinguishes left and right. The questions posed by the facilitator are never personal, but alternate between professional topics (Who likes archaeological museums? Who has ever designed a caption? Who rarely interacts with visitors?) to more light-hearted subjects (Who had coffee this morning? Who can make bread from scratch?). In addition, the same requests can be summarized on placards. Moreover, the facilitator describes verbally what is happening and how the entire group is responding to the questions. This game helps participants focus on the group's characteristics and chips away at stereotypes by showing how multifaceted people are. Ultimately, this icebreaker reveals the futility of ascribing a single label or definition to individuals.

Activity: Fantasy sport

Inspired by the VSSCH + STAM toolkit for museums, this exercise explores how to find internal allies and invites participants to reflect on their own role within the institution.[15] Participants listen to the description of a soccer field with several figures standing on it, all oriented to a goal. The facilitator helps them visualize the attacker, goalkeeper, and defender and asks each person to see themself in one of these roles. Afterward, everyone has ten to fifteen minutes for individual reflection, in which they estimate the number and types of kicks they will need to score a goal. The following feedback section is open-ended, and participants are free to share their thoughts or not.

- Materials: standard-sized paper for the worksheets
- Preparation: draw or find an image of a soccer field to be projected, featuring a goal with the word *GOAL* written on it and a drawing of some stylized players that take up the whole sheet

Role play activity

This activity is used to identify barriers in different work areas and help people perceive the vital role that collaboration plays in issues of accessibility. The participants work in pairs or groups of three who are assigned two or three typical situations in which different visitors face a given barrier. Some examples could be:

- a person who wants to visit the museum uses the website but is unable to find information about accessibility
- a visitor who approaches the reception staff without receiving useful information
- a caption that is difficult to read or understand

Each scenario represents and explains the given type of barrier (be it communicative, cognitive, sensory, etc.). This specification makes it easy for the participants to mark their assigned barrier on a large grid hung on the wall. This grid also reflects different professions and roles within the museum. Once a group has read over their example, it is invited to come up with possible solutions to the barriers. It then writes them on a Post-it that will be stuck at the intersection between the column featuring the barriers and the row of areas/professions involved.

If we take the first example listed above (a person who wants to visit the museum but on the website is unable to find information about accessibility), the barriers are communicative, meaning that the sticky notes will go in the column for communicative barriers, at the intersection with the areas relating to both communication and web design. In this case, solutions might include a website update, the addition of appropriate texts, a shared training, as well as appropriate guidelines to follow. A likely trend that will emerge is that part of the responsibility also lies with those who deal with accessibility and management. The first cohort has the opportunity to share guidelines with their colleagues, while the second can program specific training sessions and define a new protocol.

The exercise does not set out to gather solutions in a systematic manner, but rather to encourage participants to think broadly about the direct and indirect responsibilities shared by all staff. The activity wraps up with a final debrief to discuss the exercise and the validity of the proposed solutions.

- Materials: sticky notes, pens, large sheets of paper
- Preparation: on the large sheet of paper, make a grid with columns dedicated to areas/roles and rows about the many types of possible barriers, namely cognitive, sensory, motor, communicative, linguistic, economic, participation, etc.

Objectives and actions

This exercise allows participants to compare expectations and exchange possible strategies and insights that will empower them to initiate practical changes. At the

Co-design

end of the session, this aims to help participants envision their role in bolstering accessibility. The activity intends to help participants convert what they have learned during the meeting into concise goals. These might include making their museum more accessible, and promoting accessibility in other areas of work. Once defined, participants should summarize their goals in a few key phrases on a Post-it. Then they will write up a second round of notes specifying actions they will take to achieve these objectives. The facilitator can sort the Post-its into clusters to make it easier for the whole group to navigate the information. This collective set of ideas often inspires people to define new plans.

- Materials: Post-it Notes, markers, a piece of poster board
- Preparation: review activity and prepare the workshop space

FINAL THOUGHTS

Rethinking accessibility constitutes a paradigm shift that relates to products and services and permeates an organization's management processes, be it a museum or other type of institution. This change in perspective makes it possible to initiate new dynamics and experiment with fresh approaches that empower people in different roles. Training can help staff recognize that they already possess valuable skills to place visitors at the center of a museum experience.

In practice, accessibility can be a means through which the whole staff acquaint themselves more deeply with ways in which diversity, equity, and inclusion relate to visitor experience. While these fields may seem like worlds apart, they all put visitors at the center of their reflections. Moreover, organizations all benefit from group cohesion, which emerges from the kinds of shared practices, exchanges, and exercises discussed above. When collaborating with external groups, accessibility again offers an opportunity to contact a new set of people and organizations, sparking new modes of outreach and participatory planning.

NOTES

1. Mike Murawski, *Museums and Agents of Change: A Guide to Becoming a Changemaker* (Lanham, MD: Rowman & Littlefield, 2020).
2. Tina C. Nielsen and Lisa Kepinski, *Inclusion Nudges for Motivating Allies in All Organizations and Communities* (Self-published, 2020).
3. Danielle Linzer, Desi Gonzalez, and Sina Bahram, "Warhol for All: Designing an Inclusive Audio Guide and Tactile Exhibition Elements at the Andy Warhol Museum," in *Inclusive Digital Interactives: Best Practices + Research*, eds. Beth Ziebarth, Janice Majewski, Robin Marquis, and Nancy Proctor (Access Smithsonian, IHCD and MuseWeb, 2020), 243–64, https://ihcd-api.s3.amazonaws.com/s3fs-public/file+downloads/Inclusive+Digital+Interactives+Best+Practices+%2B+Research .pdf.
4. Ibid., 245.

5. Ibid., 250.

6. For more information, Emma Shepley, "Advancing Disability Equality through Cultural Institutions," Research Centre for Museums and Galleries (RCMG), *Research Impact Report*, Spring 2020, https://le.ac.uk/rcmg/reframing-difference-and-disability; Alex Marshall, "Is This the World's Most Accessible Museum?" *New York Times*, published Sept. 6, 2019, updated Sept. 11, 2019, accessed March 21, 2020, www.nytimes.com/2019/09/06/arts/design/disabled-access-wellcome-collection.html.

7. Anne Chick, "Co-creating an Accessible, Multisensory Exhibition with the National Centre for Craft & Design and Blind and Partially Sighted Participants," in *REDO: 2017 Cumulus International Conference*, 30 May–2 June 2017, Kolding Design School, Kolding, Denmark, https://eprints.lincoln.ac.uk/id/eprint/27590/1/120_long_Chick-2%20%281%29.pdf.

8. Ibid., 6.

9. Sarah Smed, "Behind Barbed Wire: Co-producing the Danish Welfare Museum," in *Museums and Social Change: Challenging the Unhelpful Museum*, eds. Adele Chynoweth, Bernadette Lynch, Klaus Petersen, and Sarah Smed (London: Routledge, 2020).

10. "Percorsi speciali," Castello D'Albertis Museo delle Culture del Mondo, accessed July 3, 2021, www.museidigenova.it/it/percorsi-speciali.

11. Ellysheva Zeira, former education specialist for access, Lower East Side Tenement Museum, interview by author, New York City, October 14, 2014.

12. Bernadette Lynch, "I'm Gonna Do Something: Moving Beyond Talk in the Museum," in *Museum Activism*, eds. Robert R. Janes and Richard Sandell (London: Routledge, 2019).

13. Marianella Sclavi and Lawrence E. Susskind, *Confronto creativo. Dal diritto di parola al diritto di essere ascoltati* (Milano et al., 2011).

14. "TV 2 | All That We Share," TV 2 PLAY, accessed July 23, 2021, http://www.youtube.com/watch?v=jD8tjhVO1Tc.

15. Erik Schilp and Jasper Visser, *Quantum Culture* (Amsterdam: VSSCH + STAM, 2018).

10

Finding Solutions

FROM PROTOTYPING TO ORGANIZATIONAL CHANGE

Accessibility means providing diverse people with equal opportunities by generating solutions that respond to their needs. These solutions often involve the removal of barriers, which are the result of numerous factors, including unawareness of their existence. Due to this ignorance, accessibility remains undervalued as a discipline. Hence, management rarely perceives, let alone proposes, accessibility as an institutional priority. As departments struggle to collaborate, their efforts lack structure and fail to cater to people's needs in effective ways. Furthermore, staff members, no matter how diverse, can never fully represent the multifaceted reality of its audience. These issues hint at shortfalls and problems that museums rarely share or even know about. By bringing these problems to light, institutions can start addressing them to explore one, small solution at a time.

The first step is context analysis, allowing museums to identify both barriers and allies; these findings guide the process that will lead to the most suitable and effective practices. Yet several factors condition these choices, including aspects like a museum's willingness to invest in accessibility, the time that can be devoted to research, the manager's coordination and design skills, the financial resources available, or the institution's propensity for change. Focusing on accessibility solutions is like a problem-solving exercise, and it starts with a brainstorming session: gather as much information as possible, get a good overview of the situation, recognize hard-to-see obstacles, and solve the more straightforward ones. This method applies to any number of areas, like the assessment of educational activities or preparing an exhibition.

It's important to start small to reach big. For example, focusing on the barriers in communication materials can be an important first step. This accessibility review of one area offers a chance to test methods that can be scaled up to more complex problem domains.

Defining priorities can be one of the most difficult things to do. When there are dozens of barriers to dismantle, a clear set of criteria indicates where to start. A medium- to long-term plan must guide the sequence and magnitude of the removal process, regardless of the budget's scope. It's also important to keep in mind that these initiatives are often aimed at people who have historically been excluded, so it is unfair to run the risk of abruptly interrupting a newly started relationship. Planning and creativity are keys. We can find support and inspiration in research and existing models, be they innovative, experimental, traditional, or the result of a co-design process. What matters most is their impact on visitors and on the whole organization.

ANALYZING BARRIERS AND BRAINSTORMING SOLUTIONS

Once the existing barriers have been accurately mapped, as discussed in chapter 8, it is time to analyze them and identify those to be removed first. Museums can thus base their decisions on a broad, yet concrete understanding of the context. With this method, it becomes easier to identify big or small barriers that can be resolved through minimal intervention. One solution that is easy to share and implement is to encourage staff positioned at a museum's entrance to be informed of existing facilities, as well as to be helpful and welcoming. Creating a priority entry for some audiences provides another simple and low-cost solution.

Since accessibility is often required by law, it is common to assume that most requirements have been met and that there are no further obligations in this regard. This ambiguity makes it difficult to identify and establish priorities for removing existing barriers. Although one decision does not preclude another, limited resources are bound to influence choices, especially in smaller museums. For a cultural organization to develop more fully, it can be helpful to receive guidance about how to proceed in the pursuit of wide-reaching and well-structured accessibility. Bringing accessibility into full effect may never be totally achieved, but this awareness should not prevent us from treating it as a fundamental goal.

Once a team has identified barriers and evaluated possible solutions, feasibility and priority set the basis on which a selection is carried out. The first of these two criteria relates to factors like time, personnel, economic resources, and the ease with which they can be carried out. The second factor relates to the degree in which a barrier's removal can impact people's experience in museums.

These elements cannot be assigned an absolute value, and our investigations must leave room for exceptions while considering specific cases and contexts. During the mapping process, it is useful to associate each type of barrier with certain indicators. These can become criteria for schematizing choices according to the Eisenhower Matrix, a decision-making tool that draws inspiration from a quote by the former US president Dwight D. Eisenhower: "I have two kinds of problems, the urgent ones and the important ones. The urgent ones are not important, and the important ones are never urgent."[1] This matrix inspired the first exercise in the workshop that will be introduced later in the chapter.

Once the actions' order and feasibility have been established, another important step is to identify which target audiences might be excluded or negatively impacted by our choices. For example, curb solutions, useful for people with visual impairments, may be an obstacle for wheelchairs: The frequency of these kinds of contrasts presents a challenge that forces us to think complexly. With this reference, this activity often highlights and prioritizes proposals especially aimed at people with disabilities, given that it is they who experience the greatest limitations.

Another significant task is to establish a strategic sequence through a well-defined series of priorities that covers all points and outlines a medium- to long-term timetable for an institution's development. This type of analysis allows staff from different areas to share their thoughts and experiences through a process managed by a team dedicated to accessibility. When this activity is carried out by a mixed group, there is a tendency to underestimate the complexity of some proposals, producing the false impression that most actions are easy and urgent. While we know there are many effective actions that can be accomplished with minimal intervention, it is important to steer clear of the pitfall of labeling everything as "easy." Hence, we need to identify what are the most urgent matters in light of feasible alternatives. As we have seen, it takes very little effort to update accessibility information on a website or in a garden, for example, to help visitors orient themselves during their visit through the sensory presence of aromatic plants.

This entire process depends on a certain level of disciplinary expertise among those involved, and most of this knowledge and these skills can be imparted. To be able to outline potential solutions, staff needs to be familiar with eminent, international case studies, the history and theory of the subject, and existing guidelines. If there is no one on staff who feels adequately qualified to do so, an external consultant can fill these gaps. It is not necessary to know everything, as consultants and networks can make all the difference. In general, the quality and range of knowledge and previous planning will determine the quality of the proposed solutions, which will reflect on the museum's accessibility and success. As previously seen, the global pandemic gave rise to several, hastily crafted digital proposals that offer clear evidence of this lack of planning. A solid understanding of the discipline will enable staff to recognize when certain barriers can be solved with elementary interventions. In many instances, simpler outcomes may prove more effective and less expensive than other, more sophisticated options.

BEST PRACTICES AS SOLUTIONS

Designing solutions does not mean reinventing the wheel. Plenty of approaches have already been devised and tested in the field. Although accessibility remains an area of ongoing research, there is a wealth of good practices and recommendations that offer models for action. The same checklists used during the barrier mapping phase, for example, can offer solutions for many aspects of the museum experience.

Good practices are those that feature programs, products, and tools that can be implemented in exhibit setup, communications, interpersonal relationships, educational activities, ticketing, and event organization. Accessibility, like many other fields, often witnesses the gradual spread of practices that have become models, and it is interesting to note the reasons for the success and international diffusion of some projects over others, which may be equally rigorous and effective. The difference often lies in excellent communication and the ability to tell the methods and the research behind a project, as with the already-mentioned MoMA Alzheimer's Project, which offers a clear example.[2]

Good practices can also come from contexts outside the museum world. Museums can draw inspiration from results achieved in the field of airport signage, or accessibility solutions adopted by some Chicago theaters. The most effective way to engage with good and best practices, however, is to experience them firsthand. It is not always possible to gauge the quality of an operation, and especially its eventual contradictions, from a distance. Exploring different experiences requires a case-by-case understanding of the most suitable solutions to adopt for each specific context.

This volume is largely inspired by the principles of inclusive design, an approach that aims to deliver experiences whose sole purpose is inclusion, regardless of ability, age, condition, or knowledge. The premise is to always try to develop solutions that ensure equal access for all, through different strategies able to provide similar opportunities to every individual. Consequently, inclusive design can take different shapes based on flexibility, such as:

1. Structuring proposals that are accessible to the widest range of conditions without the need for adaptation; and
2. Differentiating the options available to offer alternatives suited to different visitors.

Captions offer another helpful example. If they are considered inaccessible and need to be redesigned and replaced, our first concern must be to create new ones that guarantee access to a wider audience. This means reassessing their legibility, comprehensibility, content, and positioning, as well as exploring alternative formats. The process sets out to create new offerings that are as inclusive and universal as possible.

If replacing the existing captions is not an option, an alternative might be to enhance the addition of alternative tools. The combination of different media and formats also bolsters understanding by ensuring that each individual can choose the solution that suits them best. There are many possibilities to choose from, even though the key is to identify the most effective solutions on a case-by-case basis.

Educational programs deserve a separate analysis, for they are crucial to accessibility. Furthermore, certain groups and individuals can only be comfortable in the museum through the mediation of a qualified person who facilitates their experience. The relationship here primarily involves the adoption of principles based on flexibility, incentive to autonomy, and whenever possible, interaction. This awareness and these soft skills are essential to forging relationships, but it often can only be acquired through direct experience like that provided by firsthand research, observation, or training. This said, it is worth remembering how risky it is to try to replicate educational proposals after merely having read an online description. Taking inspiration from successful experiences and best practices, it is most valuable to implement solutions that stem from frank exploration, probing questions, and honest assessments.

PROTOTYPING NEW IDEAS

In the museum world and beyond, the field of accessibility offers us the possibility of creating customized projects to meet a series of precise needs. In this case, we are referring to a method through which to create innovative solutions known as prototyping. This practice is much more complex than the adoption of existing solutions and requires expertise. It entails a considerable time commitment and, above all, the possibility of carrying out trial tests before adopting a given solution.

The suggested framework again comes from the discipline of design and uses specific indications to structure a process that transforms a research path into a physical reality. Prototypes are categorized on a fidelity scale that relates to the quality of the finished product. Low fidelity connotes a project that is still in the draft stage, even as a mere sketch, while high-fidelity prototypes are much closer to the final product, also in terms of their sensory component.

The prototype production process serves as an ongoing evaluation of solutions' effectiveness. It is useful for many different operations: defining an object, workshop planning, or even exhibition design. They can all undergo intermediate front-end evaluation (carried out between conception and development) or a formative assessment (conducted between development and realization).

An interesting project to consider in this context is the one developed by the Metropolitan Museum of Art in 2013, which involved, for a semester, a group of students from the Design and Technology Program within Parsons' School of Art, Media, and Technology, together with museum education specialists, users, and access technology experts. The working group started by listening to the needs and desires of people with disabilities and went on to design innovative technologies and prototypes capable of responding to the needs that emerged.[3]

The Canadian Museum of Human Rights provides a more complex case. Its aim is to set new standards in accessibility and in its processes. This aspiration was part of the museum since its very inception and gave rise to a clear mandate that identified inclusive design as one of the museum's key features.[4] Opened in 2014, all its exhibits and services were built with inclusive design and accessibility in mind. The institution embraces design thinking from a critical and strategic perspective, "in order to ensure it wasn't just telling human rights stories, but that it was equally concerned with the manner in which these stories were being delivered."[5] The structure takes equal interest in methods and outcomes that contribute to exceptionally articulated design. These criteria stretch to all aspects of the visitor experience, including digital resources and other media: services that reflect systematic testing and prototyping. The full adoption of these approaches created a generation of innovative solutions. Although these design projects required a significant commitment of both time and energy, they offered the advantage of being highly reliable thanks to extensive design verification.

ORGANIZATION-WIDE SOLUTIONS

The inner workings of an organization have a profound impact on its relationship with the public. The adjunct role assigned to accessibility in a museum provides a salient example: This sector will inevitably have a marginal impact if there is no contact person or if it occupies the bottom of the organizational chart. By defining a point person to specifically deal with this issue, the museum appoints a spokesperson. The capacity to do so often depends on an institution's size and its legal obligations, but mostly on its existing degree of awareness. There are geographical trends that emerge; in countries like Italy or Portugal, very few museums can count on permanent staff members whose work is wholly dedicated to this topic. In most cases, the staff member dealing with accessibility does not work exclusively in this area but is often also involved in educational programs. In some cases, this approach is the result of deliberate choices: For some museums, working toward inclusivity means bolstering awareness of the needs of people with disabilities across the board and integrating these proposals into broader programs. Palazzo Strozzi in Florence offers an excellent example. This major exhibition space dealing mostly with contemporary art has no permanent collection, but its educational department develops proposals for people with disabilities on an equal basis with any other program designed for different types of visitors.[6]

Another approach is the increasingly popular option of appointing Diversity, Equity, Accessibility, and Inclusion (DEAI) managers. These are professionals whose work is entirely dedicated to these issues and whose role is to ensure inclusion and incorporate topics regarding accessibility. This approach presents both advantages and limitations compared to the propositions raised thus far, but what is most important to emphasize here is the necessity to endow this or any figure dedicated to these themes with the power to make institutional decisions.

If museums create new professional figures, they need to equip such staff members with operational functions. Failing to do so generates misunderstandings about the importance of these roles. Quoting Senge, Yuha Jung talks about "system ignorance" in museums, explaining this as the "tendency of people consistently producing the same results that are not intended and often harmful, yet not being able to fix them in a sustainable way."[7] This said, there is an increasingly widespread belief that change can only come about by working in a structured manner across multiple levels. In the 2017 report "Organizing the Work of the Art Museum," the American Association of Art Museum Directors reveals that museums are progressively working to facilitate audience engagement from an organizational point of view.[8] While this paper does not include explicit references to accessibility, it signals an emerging trend in museum organizations. It is important to understand the nature of the driving force behind this change, as well as the factors that facilitate it.

The Science Museum of Boston was already questioning these issues back in 2011, starting with a study aimed at understanding which practices and processes were able to support change and promote inclusiveness—both in the organization's inner workings and in its public offerings—with particular attention paid to people with disabilities.[9] Through the analysis of three case studies in as many scientific museums, findings suggest that change is only possible when implemented on an ongoing basis and when it is strongly structured within different areas of the organization. The Science Museum of Boston used this research to formulate general considerations designed to make the institution more inclusive through the following initiatives:

1. Involve people with disabilities in the organization's work;
2. Reach a broad range of staff members by embedding information about inclusive practices into museum communications, professional development, and large projects;
3. Engage in ongoing experimentation and reflections on inclusive practices;
4. Promote the idea that design strategies that benefit people with disabilities improve the museum experience for all audiences.[10]

The adoption of these solutions, starting with a framework driven by the specific desire to involve people with disabilities, has further strengthened the museum's commitment to the process. But what form can an organization take to maximize its ability to be inclusive? How can different models make an effective impact?

A traditional, hierarchical structure often brings advantages, especially in terms of simplifying decisions, but this kind of organization is subject to a certain rigidity and an excessive deference to those at the top of the pyramid. To mitigate these potential problems, Jim Richardson reminds us that a flatter management framework can improve museum functions. This is especially useful when trying to enhance educational activities, which means that very probably this approach can be beneficial to accessibility as well, in a broader sense.[11] In fact, this frame narrows the distance and the communications gap between decision-makers and the public. Furthermore, it means assigning equal weight to different skills: a real achievement for accessibility. If a structure rejects corporate-style verticality, it can move toward a model more akin to the one used at colleges and universities, where "academics with similar qualifications are often seen as equals even if they work in very different niches."[12]

To some extent, this approach recalls the concept of diffuse leadership mentioned earlier as one of the ways to guarantee inclusivity. It is based on the principle of sharing expertise across different areas through the diverse skills and experiences of individual staff members. Such a scheme relies on negotiation techniques and constant feedback, while reducing power tensions and favoring creative flow.[13]

FOSTERING STAFF DIVERSITY

Any evaluation of the organizational context will inevitably explore representation and staff diversification in terms of gender, sexuality, race, and disability. A survey of current managerial makeup can invite questions like: Is a group of managers and leaders with very little diversity likely to come up with innovative proposals? What degree of separation should there be between designers and users? How can we diversify the audience if the staff itself is homogeneous? And if we can, are we truly open to this change?

Ensuring staff diversity—in terms of background, needs, experience, and interests—is one of the most significant and lively debates in the museum landscape today. The reasons are obvious, both in terms of representation and advocacy. Furthermore, diversity is widely recognized as a key element in achieving more innovative solutions.

In recent years, many organizations and museums have been concerned with facilitating the entry of diverse staff and leaders. In fact, some authors have identified a link between diversity and performance levels. An essential aspect of this work involves establishing a culture of listening between staff who share similar needs and interests to the people with whom they want to establish a dialogue. Yet success in diversity management is not measured by a mere increase in the number of people who tick certain boxes or by a reduction in discrimination. Addressing diversity within organizations, senior researcher Alessandra Romano states that the first indicators of effectiveness in diversity management initiatives are:

- The organization's ability to contain stereotypes and prejudices present in the workplace;
- An ability to promote patterns of meaning that are sensitive to diversity in the people who work for and recognize themselves in that organization;
- Reduced levels of conflict;
- The perception among employees that the quality of services has improved;
- Improved levels of customer satisfaction.[14]

In essence, this involves creating contexts in which the risk of conflict is minimized while the potential for innovation and performance is enhanced, all within a system that must inevitably adapt to new values.

Here, too, it is important to keep a close eye on the stereotypes associated with race, gender, disability, and ageism, just to mention a few. As these biases and clichés diminish (also thanks to professional development workshops), museums can build up inclusive employment opportunities for people by taking their existing or potential skills into account. In the case of cognitive disabilities, for example, it would be auspicious to build a network with other institutions that can help guide and safeguard staff integration both within the museum and beyond the structure. To catalyze this process, museums need to develop a shared analysis of their contexts and a plan for professional development that fosters autonomy and growth. This plan needs to foresee tasks that allow for the periodic assessment of acquired skills and progress made. It is, therefore, essential to develop highly collaborative approaches.

With regard to diversity management, it is important to mention the controversial matter of diversity as a transversal value. People with specific identity traits are often hired to consult in their particular area of expertise; they are often charged with the protection of groups they are supposed to represent. This approach risks relegating the communities in question to a static form of involvement and could exclude them from making contributions to a broader shift in mindset and institutional structure.

In their piece from the *Harvard Business Review*, David Thomas and Robin Ely argue that we should be striving to adopt an integrative perspective.[15] The two researchers contend that advocates should not be too tightly bound to the idea of identity, like in cases where people with disabilities are hired to work mostly on accessibility. We would all benefit from abandoning the misleading idea that "the main virtue that identity groups have to offer is a knowledge of their own people."[16] What they suggest, instead, is the adoption of an integrative-type model in which diversity—an essential factor in all groups—activates a positive feedback system across all areas of museum work. This model could allow the differences among staff members to become the drivers of integration. In so doing, organizations can internalize differences among its staff and benefit from them as contributing factors to the institution's subsequent development.

THE TRAINING

This training session is dedicated to identifying solutions and is not intended to solve all existing barriers. The workshop aims to share methods that can later be applied during the solution development stage. So, the facilitator can start the presentation by sharing theoretical assumptions and delving into case studies that illustrate the multiplicity of possible solutions for promoting accessibility among different audiences. As one of our objectives is to dismantle as many clichés as possible, it is important to emphasize the complexity of this discipline while demonstrating that simple, low-cost solutions exist. Behind the scenes, the practice can appear deceptively simple when they actually require considerable time and expertise. The presentation can opt to introduce solutions in a way that recalls the linearity of the visitor journey, a tool explored earlier in the book.

Workshop Objectives

1.   Help participants establish strategies and approaches for defining urgencies and priorities
2.   Promote awareness of accessibility as a complex matter that can also have simple solutions
3.   Encourage reflection on transversal and multilevel solutions
4.   Share ideas and approaches for breaking down barriers

The Agenda

*   Introduction and agenda
*   Icebreaker
*   Presentation
*   Activities (one or two of your choice)
*   Final debrief

Running the Workshop

Icebreaker

The marshmallow challenge is a useful and familiar icebreaker that works well in this context. The group is split into subgroups of five people. In eighteen minutes, they need to make the tallest-possible freestanding structure topped with a marshmallow using only the materials provided. This exercise teaches the necessity of planning, collaboration, and coordination in the creation of a successful product, issues to tease out with the whole group in a short debrief.

*   Materials: spaghetti, sticky tape, rope, marshmallows
*   Preparation: sort twenty sticks of spaghetti, one meter of sticky tape, one meter of rope, and one marshmallow for each team

Outlining urgent priorities

In order to acquire a clear vision of urgencies and priorities, the Eisenhower Matrix offers a useful tool. This activity lends itself to testing real data as a case study in a preexisting team of colleagues, but also to a group of participants from different backgrounds. The exercise is divided into two steps, to be introduced one at a time.

The first step involves assigning barriers to participants, who are then asked to devise solutions and write them on Post-it Notes, using one Post-it Note per solution. After the exercise, the facilitator reads the proposed solutions aloud without adding further comment. In the second step, the facilitator describes a standard museum scenario that details the size of the institution, available budget, and the number of staff members dedicated to accessibility (operating under the assumption that the example chosen has no accessibility facilities currently in place): This way, participants have the opportunity to envision their proposals in a real context and, if necessary, correct them.

Participants are then asked to place their solutions within the Eisenhower Matrix according to the level of ease, difficulty, urgency, or possibility to postpone. Once all the Post-it Notes have been placed on the board, the facilitator will review the activity and assess the participants' evaluation of the solutions. It is useful to dedicate time to talking about the complexities of certain choices.

At the end of the exercise, it is also helpful to draw the participants' attention to the usefulness of this approach when defining the order in which to carry out actions. Those to be tackled first are the easiest and most urgent, while the difficult or deferrable ones are hardest to put into practice, take time, and come later.

- Materials: different-colored Post-it Notes, markers, sheet/board
- Preparation: the facilitator should make a list of real or hypothetical barriers (perhaps those identified in a previous workshop), prepare two sets of different-colored Post-it Notes, and draw a Cartesian plane on a large sheet of paper or board on which the terms "Easy" and "Difficult" are placed at opposite ends of the y-axis and "Urgent" and "Postponable" are placed on either end of the x-axis. The sheet/board should be large enough to hold all the Post-its distributed to the participants.

UX storyboard

Exploring the journey experience can become a useful exercise to verify the efficacy of a prototype—be it a product or experience—when it takes the form of a storyboard. Workshop participants are divided into groups, each of which is assigned an imaginary visitor. The facilitator provides some input about the visitor, whose characteristics are then fleshed out by the group. Using Post-it Notes, each group maps the experience through the perspective of their fictional visitor by considering questions raised and modes of interaction encountered during the visit. It is also important to imagine the ways in which a visitor might recount their experiences retrospectively.

A series of sketches illustrates steps that will then be presented to the entire group when it reconvenes. After each presentation, other participants will have the chance to bring up any gaps in the journey or add observations to supplement each experience. At the end of the activity, all the raised ideas can be collected in a report and used to adjust the initial prototype.

FINAL THOUGHTS

The search for accessibility solutions calls on a vast range of resources and invites us to rethink transformation processes in pursuit of new models. Museums have often adopted standardized solutions, only to realize that visitors are more complex than they had initially realized. The strategies for cultivating new awareness are manifold. Research in the field of accessibility, in turn, stimulates greater understanding. Accessibility, as stated time and again, weaves through organizations to differing degrees and can be applied in more or less traditional ways; the achieved outcomes and impacts inevitably reciprocate the level of commitment and flexibility employed.

NOTES

1. This sentence was originally pronounced by Roscoe Miller, president of Northwestern University (Evanston, IL). It became famous in 1954, when Eisenhower repeated it during a speech to the Second Assembly of the World Council of Churches.
2. "Meet Me at MoMA: The MoMA Alzheimer's Project," Museum of Modern Art (MoMA), accessed June 9, 2021, https://www.moma.org/visit/accessibility/meetme/.
3. "A Museum for Everyone," New School, accessed June 20, 2021, https://www.newschool.edu/pressroom/pressreleases/2013/ParsonsandTheMetropolitanMuseumofArt.htm.
4. "Toward Greater Inclusion and Equity," Canadian Museum of Human Rights, accessed June 21, 2021, https://humanrights.ca/about/toward-greater-inclusion-and-equity.
5. Bruce Wyman, Corey Timpson, Scott Gillam, and Sina Bahram, "Inclusive Design: From Approach to Execution," *MW2016: Museums and the Web 2016*, February 24, 2016, accessed June 30, 2021, https://mw2016.museumsandtheweb.com/paper/inclusive-design-from-approach-to-execution.
6. Irene Balzani, head of accessibility projects and family activities, Palazzo Strozzi, interview by author, Florence (Italy), February 26, 2020.
7. Yuha Jung, "Toward a Learning Museum and System Intelligence," in *System Thinking in Museums: Theory and Practice*, eds. Yuha Jung and Ann Rowson Love (Lanham, MD: Rowman & Littlefield, 2017), 229.
8. Roger Schonfeld and Liam Sweeney, "Organizing the Work of the Art Museum," in *Ithaka S+R*, last modified July 10, 2019, accessed June 10, 2021, https://doi.org/10.18665/sr.311731.
9. Beth Malandain et al., "An Ongoing Experiment: Developing Inclusive Digital Interactives at a Science Museum," in *Inclusive Digital Interactives: Best Practices + Research*, eds. Beth Ziebarth, Janice Majewski, Robin Marquis, and Nancy Proctor (Access Smithsonian, IHCD and MuseWeb, 2020), 60, https://ihcd-api.s3.amazonaws.

com/s3fs-public/file+downloads/Inclusive+Digital+Interactives+Best+Practic-
es+%2B+Research.pdf.
10. Ibid., 61–63.
11. Jim Richardson, "Can Flatter Organisational Structures Work for Museums?" in *Museum Next*, October 23, 2019, accessed April 21, 2021, www.museumnext.com/article/can-flatter-organisational-structures-work-for-museums/.
12. Ibid.
13. Alessandra Romano, *Diversity and Disability Management: Esperienze di inclusione sociale* (Milano: Mondadori, 2020), 20.
14. Ibid., 7–8.
15. David A. Thomas and Robin J. Ely, "Making Difference Matter: A New Paradigm for Managing Diversity," in *On Diversity*, ed. *Harvard Business Review* (Boston: Harvard Business Review Press, 2019).
16. Ibid., 2.

11

From Evaluation to Strategic Planning

Once access solutions have been defined, institutions and staff are often satisfied with preliminary results, but it is important to continue stoking the process and keep sight of long-range goals. Experience shows that the gratification of having achieved something is no guarantee that tasks have been carried out correctly. The only way to ascertain the true value of our actions is to listen to the opinions of those on the receiving end. This process differs from the long-term nature of co-design discussed in earlier chapters. Instead, it is advisable to evaluate individual moments and occasions through questions that are carefully tailored to the situation. This form of assessment serves, for the most part, as an opportunity to verify each stage of a project in relation to the needs and thoughts of its beneficiaries. Evaluations are crucial to organizational learning, and they must be carefully designed to elicit the most pertinent information. By implementing these findings into their work, organizations confirm their willingness to change and to involve a broad range of agents from the evaluation stage.

Improving and establishing a clear framework for a museum's development process necessarily informs strategic plans and their requirements. To draw up an effective accessibility plan, we need to look at the future from an operational perspective so as to identify the most appropriate form our choices can take. Evaluation and definition of the strategic plan, from this point of view, are two complementary and essential phases. Unfortunately, both are often underestimated, but when correctly implemented they can serve as a litmus test to determine the quality of planning. They also reveal a great deal about the skills in place, the value that is assigned to accessibility, and the commitment made to bringing it about.

EVALUATION

In previous chapters, evaluation emerged as a tool for museum self-assessment that can verify the application and correct use of certain guidelines. In some countries, current legislation stipulates the need for completing self-assessment forms, often in conjunction with the drafting of an action plan.

Whether in a museum or elsewhere, it is important to clarify what lens has been adopted to discuss these issues as well as the motivations for the evaluation. Specific needs and goals inevitably drive and influence an assessment process, so no evaluation offers fully objective results. For instance, the information that an accessibility coordinator wants to verify may be very different from that of a donor or an external policymaker. An accessibility coordinator's interest likely revolves around the impact of their projects, donors might be more focused on the way in which the museum has responded to their requests, and a policymaker may want to know if the actions implemented resonate with political priorities.[1]

What remains constant is that various pieces of knowledge are not only valuable information, but also a way to strengthen the dialogue with the visitors. Evaluations often produce knowledge related to existing and potential museum audiences, the ways they use the institution, their propensity to consume what is offered, their level of satisfaction with the experience, and more. A few years back, Harriet Foster, evaluation officer for the East of England Museum Hub, included the following list of possible evaluation objectives:

- Determine if a project or activity's aims, objectives, and outcomes are being or have been met;
- Enable us to understand our visitors/users or non-visitors/non-users better (being more user-focused) and improve the services we offer them;
- Identify strengths and weaknesses (and where resources should be directed in the future);
- Ensure that learning is shared and acted upon within the organization;
- Define the quality of what we do;
- Anticipate problems that can be resolved early on;
- Strengthen accountability and motivate staff and users;
- Demonstrate the impact of the organization to funders.[2]

These criteria are perfectly relevant to assessing accessibility, and museums can use this list to ascertain the effectiveness of proposals in this area.

In general, it is essential for an evaluation to be carefully designed and based on a clear definition of the assessment's purpose and expectations, and the already-existing data should also be considered. To this end, we can use a few questions to focus our attention on core issues: What do you want to evaluate? Why do you want to evaluate it? What will you do with the results? How important is it to know this information? It is, of course, helpful to remember that information is truly useful when it is relevant to driving decisions and actions.

More traditional literature on the topic divides the main steps into "front-end evaluation," "formative evaluation," and "summative evaluation," depending on the design stage at which the audience is involved. Front-end evaluation is carried out during the conception phase, at the very beginning of a project (for example, an exhibition) and is an effective tool for gathering people's expectations and identifying targets. It often overlaps with consultation, as intended in participatory settings, allowing people to be involved at a very early stage of the process in which they are mainly confronted with concepts. Formative evaluation, on the other hand, determines the functionality of prototypes or simulation models (as in the case of an app) and helps organizations understand audiences' reactions and usage behaviors. This stage of evaluation makes it possible to analyze the accessibility and usability of the project in question. A few years ago, the Science Museum of Boston and the association Art Beyond Sight released a study of this type of evaluation.[3] The guide offers tips for soliciting feedback on accessibility, aimed particularly at participants who are blind or visually impaired. It provides a thorough and specific question bank that can be used for this purpose.

Perhaps the best-known and most widely used approach is the summative evaluation. It takes place once the project design is complete and allows for the evaluation of different components that are less evident during earlier phases, such as in-flow analysis, which can only be carried out after a pathway has been defined; this stage also allows an institution to verify that given objectives have been achieved. However, Christian Heath and Maurice Davies, two experts from King's College London, point out that "many summative evaluations seem to set out to demonstrate success, rather [than] take an honest critical stance."[4] While not every project needs to implement all three evaluation stages, it is advisable for larger projects to alternate between the different forms to cater to different objectives.

Regardless of the evaluation's timing, it is important to institute a thorough planning process by first identifying which information is already available and then defining what objectives to achieve, methods to employ, and audiences to address. When choosing the most suitable type of inquiry and tools for the task, we need to answer these initial questions and understand the indicators of success (i.e., the elements that demonstrate whether or not an outcome has been achieved). Common examples of indicators are participation rates, individual behaviors, or attitudes.

WHICH EVALUATION STRATEGIES?

It is important to decide between qualitative and quantitative surveys. In most cases, it may prove necessary to opt for the former or to adopt a mixed method, as both of these approaches allow us to gather detailed knowledge regarding the *how* and the *why*. When dealing with accessibility, the participant sample we choose has a significant impact on the evaluation. Not only do we need to give priority to individuals who can encounter more limitations than others, but we must also bear in mind that no group has homogeneous characteristics, needs, interests, or skills. Moreover, user evaluations alone may not provide sufficient proof of accessibility, as when websites are assessed for their ability to meet shared standards. In this case, it is also necessary to involve an expert who can carry out a heuristic evaluation or make use of a standard checklist.

Once the aims, recipients, and type of research have been defined, we can turn our attention to the most suitable tools of assessment. As with any evaluation, these may be used in combination; it is also advisable to rely on a triangulation system that brings together a variety of research methods to cross-check our findings. For example, a predominantly quantitative approach, like a questionnaire, can be supplemented using qualitative tools, such as focus groups, which are better suited for investigating more complex issues like experiences or motivations. Further insight also emerges from the study of relevant literature on the topic. Triangulation applies not only to the range of methods employed, but also to the use of results gathered at different times, or in the comparison of work produced by different researchers.

When thinking about methods of carrying out audience surveys, first it is helpful to identify *internal data*. This term refers to a set of information found on a variety of media and across different levels of the organization, including data on admissions, pricing, booking, registered visits, and visitor information gathered online, as well as input from frontline staff. This information is often left untapped, despite its great potential as a learning resource. Just think of the role of museum guardians; they are in constant contact with visitors and could play an important role in the process. If properly trained, their insight into visitor behavior could provide a wealth of information about the accessibility of the institution.

It is also important to distinguish between primary and secondary sources on the basis of whether or not the organization obtained data for a specific purpose. Primary sources include questionnaires, interviews, focus groups, and observational surveys, methods that each have advantages and disadvantages when taken individually, but which collectively allow us to enter into direct dialogue with our stakeholders. When choosing the best tools, we need to identify the most effective way to gather the information we want to obtain. Each of these tools can then take on a more or less complex form. A classic example is the use of postcards on which people are asked to respond freely to a broad question, perhaps even offering a drawing to illustrate their response. A very different approach is the use of observational research, in which behavior is observed and recorded or gathered through an administered questionnaire. In other cases, an interviewer guides the respondent through a series of questions, point by point. Secondary sources, on the other hand, include statistical data from research institutes or studies carried out by public or private organizations reporting information and phenomena that relate to a broader context, pointing out issues worthy of further investigation. Overall, data collection is only an intermediate process, which must then be followed by careful analysis and interpretation before any conclusions are drawn.

In order to begin tackling these issues, we can start by examining any event and then build an evaluation process around it, as suggested by the toolkit created by Of/By/For All.[5] This resource was specially built to help carry out "respectful audience surveying," while other useful and free publications available online include Evaluation Toolkit for Museum Practitioners and Europeana Toolkit.[6]

RISKS AND SOLUTIONS: FOR ETHICAL AND ACCESSIBLE EVALUATION

When it comes to evaluation, there are certain missteps that pose notably greater risks than others. Poorly defined objectives and sloppy planning prove the biggest stumbling blocks of all. Making mistakes in these areas can result in problems that then affect all other parts of the process, from sample choices made to the method of evaluation.

Failing to include the staff in the process is another common pitfall. Adequate training helps colleagues learn how to involve each other and how to avoid wasting resources and institutional potential. Time and again, we have seen how valuable the input of staff can be. Teamwork helps ensure that information is not transmitted in a superficial or faulty manner; doing so runs the risk of undermining the evaluation's results.

It is equally important to keep the ethics of evaluation in mind. Evaluators should always value people's skills and consistently seek out user-centered solutions. One mistake that museums sometimes make is to solicit feedback solely from caregivers, excluding people with cognitive disabilities even when they are the main recipients of a given project. It could appear more convenient to address caregivers alone, because this option requires less time and attention for accessible assessment strategies. That said, this shortcut is neither a desirable nor a correct solution. There is a wealth of available tools to facilitate access in the evaluation phases, including case studies describing projects that have employed analogous strategies. To give just one example, when working with people suffering from dementia (even outside the museum context), it is customary to use tools like the smiley-face rating scale, oftentimes related to live or recorded observations, which allow evaluators to monitor behaviors of interest.

Furthermore, failing to identify strategies that allow for direct involvement of the target audience makes it impossible to ensure adequate representation. Stephanie Downey sees this as a critical issue and stresses how important it is for museums to include "visitor abilities in the standard background/demographic questions,"[7] a suggestion that is certainly helpful for gaining some understanding of the museum's propensity for and perception of accessibility. Open-ended questions are especially useful in this case. An inaccessible museum is unlikely to have visitors with disabilities, but if the institution has no access to such data, it is difficult to confirm this condition. Therefore, Downey also suggests including a deliberate sample of people with disabilities and not to rely on random sampling, regardless of whether the sample is representative of its target audience.

Upstream, another possible approach to understand what people's needs might be is to ask what accommodations they could find useful. This allows museums to avoid asking how someone identifies. Information can be collected by asking open questions or by sharing a list of possible facilities. It is always important to leave space for further comments.

Yet what tools should be used to make the assessment accessible? Various scholars have pointed out a bias generated by the inaccessibility of the methods used, meaning that some people are prevented from participating in research altogether. There is literature on this subject that insists on the importance of evaluation accessibility, highlighting a few fundamental aspects to consider in every situation, especially when the targets in question are those people with different kinds of disabilities and impairments. This observation presents at least two implications: firstly, that the chosen method must be as accessible as possible; secondly, that the chosen methods must be suitable for the purposes of the evaluation. Think, for instance, of a written questionnaire assigned to a group of children or to people with visual impairments; this tool does not constitute the most appropriate solution to use in either case. It would consequently generate bias due to the non-response of the groups in question.

There are many factors to consider when preparing an evaluation's text and format, including its impact on the participants. We need to consider the possibility of carrying out preventive tests to gauge the comprehensibility and readability of written texts. It is also important to anticipate the need for alternative formats like digital forms, but it is preferable to offer a variety of solutions over a single method. For some respondents, an interview or questionnaire might work better if administered remotely, perhaps supported by web chat or subtitles. In focus groups or interviews, it is also important to be mindful of the time people are given to respond and in so doing demonstrate respect for different needs. In general, it is worthwhile to think about what to offer interviewees through some form of compensation or benefit as a way of thanking them for their valuable time, knowledge, and input.

DEFINING AN ACCESSIBILITY PLAN

Any strategic plan for accessibility needs to integrate two essential aspects, namely ways to evaluate activities and ways to monitor the ongoing evaluation of activities. The term *accessibility plan* refers to a document that guarantees the institutional adoption of a series of choices to ensure greater accessibility. Starting with a self-diagnosis of the barriers (as described in chapter 8), this plan outlines the route to achieving these goals within a given timeframe, usually over a span of about three years. It therefore serves a vital role by presenting accessibility as a shared and achievable objective.

Unfortunately, museums do not always prioritize accessibility at the strategic level. In this regard, it is interesting to note that many institutions seem primarily interested in engaging consultants for training purposes rather than for strategic development. While this choice can be motivated by economic reasons, accessibility cannot be tethered exclusively to the present without a longer-term perspective.

Methodologies for strategy plans do not originate in the museum world, and their scope is steadily widening to encompass not only accessibility, but also issues such as diversity, inclusion, and equity. Indeed, some museums include accessibility within a broader strategic plan that addresses these concerns more holistically. However, institutions whose plan focuses entirely on issues of access can facilitate a systemic, contextual analysis and establish a clear, future-oriented plan. This plan should be a living document, to be updated by a number of professional figures, principally the director and the accessibility coordinator, but also the human resources manager and other staff responsible for the public. The Portuguese association Aceso Cultura recently published an online guide that summarizes key points for the creation of an action plan. Their suggestions involve the following areas:

- Mission of the cultural organization
- Institutional philosophy with regard to accessibility
- Responsibilities of the person charged with coordinating accessibility
- Short-, medium-, and long-term priorities
- Specific goals
- Specific actions to fulfill each goal
- Budget for carrying out each action
- Timeframe for each action
- Communications plan to announce accessibility services and improvements
- Training and professional development for permanent, temporary, and voluntary team members.[8]

As there is no standardized model for this plan, each institution's strategic plan may include other information relating to context analysis, existing challenges, and strategic tools. Or it could feature an in-depth analysis of museum policy, identifying the terms in use, the museum's commitment, and relevant regulations.

The American National Endowment for the Arts provides further guidance on this topic in its already-cited *Accessibility Planning and Resource Guide for Cultural Administrators*.[9] Their indications offer more general examples that relate to the museum field, although not exclusively. They are, nonetheless, consistent with the ADA.

Once an institution has clearly defined its goals, it is essential to outline indicators for measuring success, like those outlined above for the evaluation. The Museum of Contemporary Art Australia provides a noteworthy example. Its "Celebrating Difference: Access, Diversity and Inclusion Plan 2018–2020" defines their indicators of success in the following ways:

- Increase in the percentage of people with access requirements visiting the MCA, including participation in mainstream activity determined through audience research activity;

- Positive feedback from visitors to the Museum, access program participants and their extended network of families, carers, and disability support providers, disability organizations, and audience satisfaction surveys regarding the quality of access at MCA;
- Increase in number of MCA programs that embrace inclusive strategies;
- Increased number of employees with disability;
- Increased employment opportunities created through internship and work experience programs for people with disability and for those from disadvantaged backgrounds;
- Reviewed and improved policies and internal practices related to promoting diversity and inclusion in the workplace;
- Delivered training to all staff;
- Positive feedback from MCA employees on our diversity and inclusion approach, practices, and culture.[10]

Australia offers another interesting set of strategies laid out by the Australian Museum where the director and CEO, Kim McKay, declared that "the AM's new Accessibility and Inclusion Action Plan 2018–21 (AIAP) builds on the former Disability Inclusion Action Plan (2015–17), shifting the focus to social and physical inclusion rather than disability. Our goal is to create social change, which changes the perception and behavior toward our visitors and staff living with disability."[11] Hence, the plan not only details objectives, a legislative framework, the museum's history, and existing elements, but also cites social impact among its primary goals. The AM has extended its desired outcomes well beyond the museum threshold, to include:

- Changing community attitudes toward people with disabilities;
- Boosting community participation;
- Increasing employment opportunities for people with disability;
- Removing barriers to systems and processes.

Each of these issues is backed up by an action plan that, in addition to the timeframe for development, clearly establishes staff responsibilities in relation to each action, thus providing a concrete course of action for their involvement and development. Once an accessibility plan has been established, the hope is that it will be disseminated both internally and externally, as in the case of organizations that have shared their plan online, offering stimulus and inspiration to other institutions.

THE TRAINING

To deepen issues relating to evaluation and strategic planning, this training session is designed to help participants grapple with questions about the future of accessibility and the need to rely on specific, reliable information. The activities, therefore, are more structured and take longer than those presented in previous chapters. It is certainly useful to set up simulations to understand evaluation principles and to periodically analyze which tools are most effective. The following exercises, however, largely focus on the strategic dimension and assess the impact of certain choices. There are many ways of approaching these topics, and it is well worth consulting a resource developed by the American Alliance of Museums, namely discussion points and the questions from a Watch & Talk event dedicated to the DEAI field (made available as a summarized transcription).[12]

Workshop Objectives

1. Share principles and essential steps in making evaluations, prompting planning, and taking concrete action
2. Stimulate critical knowledge and awareness corroborated by research
3. Invite participants to think in strategic and visionary terms

The Agenda

- Introduction and agenda
- Icebreaker
- Presentation
- Activity
- Final debrief

Running the Workshop

Icebreaker

This icebreaker activity uses travel as a metaphor to help participants engage in an informal conversation about future prospects and how to monitor them. To do so, the facilitator describes and draws a large airplane (or ship) in the middle of a sheet of paper and asks some key questions: *Where have we come from? Whom are we traveling with? Whom have we forgotten? What fuels us? Who is leading the journey?* And most importantly: *Where are we going?* Participants can respond to whichever questions they like by writing their responses on Post-it Notes or answering verbally. Once all the responses have been given, it is up to the facilitator to sort the Post-its into clusters and then share a summary of the answers with the group.

- Materials: a piece of posterboard, different-colored Post-it Notes, pens, and markers
- Preparation: not required

Activity: Kwhl Table

Kwhl Table builds on themes from the icebreaker in a more structured exercise. This activity makes use of a graphic organizer that allows users to sort knowledge according to what the group *knows* (K), what they *want* to know (W), *how* they will find the information (H), and what they have *learned* (L) about a topic. This training session produces a table that participants can later use to reflect on their audience research. The exercise draws on responses gathered during the initial brainstorming activity and asks participants to interrogate evaluation methods and sources more thoroughly. It is carried out in sequential stages, with questions asked one at a time. Participants are invited to read and answer only one question at a time. If you are working with staff from a single museum, the activity can be made more challenging by dividing participants into different groups and allowing them to compare answers only at the end of the exercise.

- Materials: big sheet of paper, markers
- Preparation: divide the sheet of paper into four columns, where the questions will be written as you ask them

Activity: Gap analysis

Gap analysis is a methodology that helps teams compare expectations with the reality of the situation/set of results. It helps participants compare intermediate strategies and approaches that will allow them to achieve the desired outcome. The first step is to divide participants into subgroups of three people and ask them to discuss the aspects of their work that relate to accessibility and are worthy of investigation, like initiatives that may have received public criticism or have been proved inefficient. So, participants need to identify existing problems associated with accessibility and provide a concise written account of them on Post-it Notes that are then placed in a column on the far left of a poster. The facilitator's job will then be to discard eventual duplicates and read out the full list.

The second step is to define the long-term goals, imagining that all existing and mentioned difficulties have been solved. This step is carried out in the same way as the first, preferably using Post-it Notes of a different color than the first set and placing them on the far right of the sheet. It is important that the current status and the objectives are expressed in concrete terms.

In the third and final phase, the participants can begin to think about the gap between them and the steps needed to move from one side to the other. Participants are now free to brainstorm and fill in Post-its individually before sticking them to the poster. The facilitator will only step in at the end to select the most appropriate suggestions, which will then be used to create an action plan that lays out responsibilities, timing, and methodologies point by point.

- Materials: a piece of posterboard, different-colored Post-it Notes, pens, and markers
- Preparation: sort Post-its into two sets, corresponding to the first step and the second step of the exercise

FINAL THOUGHTS

Every choice can be and must be oriented toward development and change; when the whole staff at all levels understands this orientation, they imbue the entire organization with greater awareness. Evaluation and planning thus empowers the staff, providing them with a body of expertise founded on solid data. Through professional development, the museum acquires vital information that informs a planning process tailored to people and their needs. Some procedures risk being merely cosmetic, but the adoption of systematic measures can strengthen an organization's proactive attitude and its long-term commitment to bona-fide change.

NOTES

1. Alessandro Bollo, *Il museo e la conoscenza del pubblico: gli studi sui visitatori* (Bologna: Istituto per i Beni artistici, culturali e naturali, 2004), https://online.ibc.regione.emilia-romagna.it/I/libri/pdf/bollo.pdf.
2. Harriet Foster, *Evaluation Toolkit for Museum Practitioners* (Norwich: East of England Museum Hub, 2008), 14–15, https://visitors.org.uk/wp-content/uploads/2014/08/ShareSE_Evaltoolkit.pdf.
3. "Guide to Conducting Formative Evaluation on Accessible Programming," Museum of Science of Boston and Art Beyond Sight, November 2013, accessed June 18, 2021, www.artbeyondsight.org/mei/formative-evaluation-of-accessible-programming/.
4. Christian Heath and Maurice Davies, "Why Evaluation Doesn't Measure Up," *Museum Journal*, June 2012, www.museumsassociation.org/museums-journal/opinion/2012/06/01062012-why-evaluation-doesnt-measure-up/#.
5. "Who's Coming? Respectful Audience Surveying Toolkit," Of/By/For All, accessed June 23, 2021, https://static1.squarespace.com/static/5a8e0a68f9a61e43fb3eb0e2/t/5d0cf607a5ad8200016a8b06/1561130515568/OFBYFOR_ALL_Respectful_Audience_Surveying_Toolkit.pdf.
6. Foster, *Evaluation Toolkit*; Harry Verwayen, Julia Fallon, Julia Schellenberg, and Panagiotis Kyrou, eds., *Impact Playbook for Museums, Libraries, Archives, and Galleries* (Den Haag: Europeana Foundation, 2017).
7. Stephanie Downey, "Five Ways Evaluators Can Further Accessibility Efforts in Museums," *RK&A Learn with Us*, July 20, 2020, accessed June 18, 2021, https://rka-learnwithus.com/five-ways-evaluators-can-further-accessibility-efforts-in-museums/.
8. Hugo Sousa and Maria Vlachou, *The Cultural Participation of People with Disabilities or Impairments: How to Create an Accessibility Plan* (Lisbon: Cámara Municipal, 2020), 49, https://accesscultureportugal.files.wordpress.com/2021/03/manual_access_plan.pdf.

9. "Develop an Access Plan in Accessibility Planning and Resource Guide for Cultural Administrators," National Endowment for the Arts, 2011, accessed June 22, 2021, www.arts.gov/sites/default/files/Step7.pdf.
10. "Celebrating Difference: Access, Diversity and Inclusion Plan 2018–2020," Museum of Contemporary Art Australia, accessed June 22, 2021, https://www.mca.com.au/about-us/reports-and-policies/access-diversity-and-inclusion-plan-20182020/.
11. "Accessibility and Inclusion Action Plan 2018–2021: Providing Accessible and Inclusive Exhibits, Programs and Services," Australian Museum, accessed June 22, 2021, https://media.australian.museum/media/dd/documents/australian-museum-accessibility-and-inclusion-action-plan-2018-2021-v2.77da658.pdf.
12. "Evaluation in Diversity, Equity, Accessibility, and Inclusion Work: Lessons Learned from Museum Professionals Watch & Talk Host Guidelines," American Alliance of Museums, https://www.aam-us.org/wp-content/uploads/2019/07/Evaluation-in-DEAI-Work-host-guidelines-1.pdf.

12

What's Next?

Those working in accessibility hope there will come a time when it is no longer necessary to make its existence explicit. The goal is for accessibility to become automatic, universally present, and considered a given—as much as possible. Access has been compared to safety: Before entering a building, we never stop to check if it is safe to do so. We simply assume our safety is guaranteed. For those who are unfamiliar with the subject, discovering accessibility and its potential often comes as an epiphany: They suddenly realize that audiences have a plethora of unrecognized needs, outright necessities that can sometimes be addressed through quite simple solutions.

With a focus on the impact and lessons this discipline offers, this closing chapter seeks to address various, ancillary aspects that are prerequisites for spreading accessibility. We hope to contribute to spark a multiplicity of new possibilities, perspectives, and methods by fostering a critical understanding of the subject's complexities and challenges. In order to bring this about, however, we need to act as spokespeople to ensure that accessibility is talked about, understood, and valued. For the same reasons, it is vital that we seek out sounding boards and networks that can amplify our work and encourage improvement through debate and exchange. We also need to continue keeping tabs on dominant perceptions throughout all areas of the organization and pay greater attention to the way needs overlap each other so our actions can activate and model social change.

SPREAD THE WORD

Communication is everything in the museum world, and the correlation between effective communication and accessibility is often very tight. Taking a broad view, we can observe ways in which internal and external channels of communication serve to spread awareness and knowledge of this issue. The choices we make in this area can have a domino effect on an institution's dialogue between leaders, staff, and volunteers, as well as on their interactions with users, visitors, and citizens in general. Although the purpose and messages vary depending on the intended recipient of the communication, what remains constant is the need to portray this issue as vital and indispensable, and to provide timely and accessible information about the programs and initiatives offered. Internally, this means ensuring a constant flow of information about the ongoing situation to ensure that all staff stay up-to-date. Oftentimes, this kind of communication is only addressed to those in charge, so that only they are aware of work being done. Instead, it is important for this information to be shared throughout the organization, starting with visitor services, frontline staff, and security.

The National Center on Disability and Access to Education (NCDAE) also stresses the importance of communicating about issues of accessibility as an ongoing process.[1] For them, rather than sharing everything in a single annual training session, it is much more helpful to provide staff with periodic updates. There are many issues that need to be included in this endeavor, and the NCDAE suggests regularly sharing about the following areas:

- Responsibilities/accountability procedures
- Scope of the plan: What will be affected?
- Fiscal and personnel support available
- Training and learning support mechanisms
- Timelines/milestones
- Feedback mechanisms
- Assessment/evaluation plans[2]

It could also be useful to set up a small publication or to publish updates on existing channels. These outlets help disseminate knowledge on more technical issues and complement more traditional training. In addition, these materials can be made available to a range of online readers. The ultimate goal is to create a culture of accessibility in which all staff understand the importance of considering people's different needs. This belief also needs to translate into practice by making presentations accessible and knowing how to relate to diverse audiences appropriately.

Communication with the public is critical and must be made up of a series of technical choices designed to maximize readability and comprehensibility, while effectively using social media and the institution's website. A flawless proposal aimed at visitors is unlikely to be effective if poorly communicated: It will not reach the people for whom it was intended and will serve as an illustration of the museum's inability to communicate both in theory and practice. More specifically, proper strategies may include integrating accessibility services in a range of promotional materials that include the web but stretch even further. For example, a brochure can be a very effective way to share about accessibility services or to present different proposals to targeted groups.

We also need to pay attention to the aesthetic component of certain accessibility programs or initiatives communication. Well-presented materials are especially important when trying to include traditionally excluded groups. Not doing so is a dangerous error and unwittingly sends the message that intended recipients merit sloppy attention.

NETWORKING

A scaled implementation of accessibility programs involves institutionalized networks. The creation of a network, most often on a territorial basis, offers the advantage of allowing members to grow together. If the exchange is open and honest, everyone benefits from both the successes and the mistakes of others. It is well worth the effort to create space for regular exchange that includes opportunities for training and refresher courses.

The MAC (Museum, Arts and Culture Access Consortium) in New York sets a good example.[3] Beyond acting as a platform for accessibility representatives at various museums, it enables people working in the discipline to keep in touch and exchange ideas and news. The organization collects all available accessibility programs in a single online calendar, providing professionals and the public with an invaluable resource. As mentioned in the chapter about digital tools, the group recently carried out a study into digital and accessible approaches and provides very useful tools that further enhance the already plentiful offerings in this section of its website.

The Chicago Cultural Accessibility Consortium (CCAC) in Chicago also works at the intersection of complementary needs to acquire skills and ideas for mutual development.[4] This exchange unites professionals from a range of cultural organizations, such as arts centers, theaters, and museums, and it offers a considerable catalog of online and in-person training opportunities. Their communication is exemplary and offers relevant news through the consortium's website and social media. Another one of their noteworthy proposals is the CCAC's equipment loan program that allows museums and theaters to loan accessible equipment at no cost to them. This removes a barrier to providing accessible services, as cost is usually the primary reason for not providing accessible offerings.

Partnerships can extend across different sectors and institutions, with museums potentially finding opportunities to grow, along with other organizations like universities or associations with specific areas of expertise. In Tuscany (Italy), there is an excellent network of organizations, called *Musei Toscani per l'Alzheimer* (Tuscan Museums for Alzheimer's), working with people living with dementia and their caregivers, which was developed through the cooperation between various figures from museums, members of civil society, and experts.[5] This community not only ensures that participants have access to advanced training opportunities (including recent international conferences), but it is also working to include museum proposals in the network of social and public health services. This partnership is the fruit of much dialogue between experts in the cultural and sanitary sector and policymakers, and it is making an impact on region-wide political strategies. This example testifies to ways in which networking allows people to remain up-to-date, while helping experts organize structured programs and workshops that are unique, consistent, not redundant, and, hence, effective.

CORRECT PERCEPTIONS OF DISABILITY

In countries where there is already a public discourse around the issue of equity and equality, there have been numerous initiatives, many of them grassroots in origin, urging museums to interrogate themselves about ways they assume exclusive and singular narratives. This is particularly true for people with disabilities, because subtle cues reinforce the common stereotype that promotes the perception of a homogenous group of placid people who lack autonomy. We risk inadvertently perpetuating clichés that are in urgent need of reversal, even in the framework of inclusive design.

To understand the way in which stereotypes and clichés are conveyed, we need only consider the symbols used to represent disability around the world. Most of us are familiar with the icon showing a white person in a motionless wheelchair against a blue background. Compare this with the Dynamic Accessibility Symbol developed in the United States in 2001, depicting a person sitting in a wheelchair while driving it forward. The latter version of the symbol insists on the subject's dynamism and autonomy and can easily be found online via the Accessible Icon Project, defined as "an ongoing work of design activism."[6] Though apparently similar, the two images reveal starkly different views of disability.

The contrast between the two icons reminds us how rhetoric can represent or misrepresent disability. Museums can generate opposing ideas through their choice of designs because they, like all institutions, run the risk of perpetuating existing stereotypes. Museums, however, have a unique power to tear them down and cultivate greater awareness. A more correct approach probably promotes normalization and insists on a neutral tone. This message is automatically altered when projects dedicated to accessibility are labeled as "special": a dangerous and recurring word choice that emphasizes the differences between someone who is considered "normal" in contrast to someone with a condition that culturally diverges from that norm.

This is why recalibrating the hierarchy of accessibility practices entails rethinking disability itself. For example, tactile experiences are often considered compensatory measures reserved solely for visitors with visual disabilities when they, in fact, serve all audiences. Or take, for instance, a museum's decision to exhibit work created by a group of adults with cognitive disabilities. A given museum may not necessarily be the right place to display these pieces, but if it is, we must hope there is a mindful curator with the necessary expertise driving the exhibit and developing itineraries free from biases. While they exist, we do not really need museums about disability, but rather museums with the capacity to showcase the differences between diverse learning styles and sensory channels, while presenting them as equally valid. So, instead of a museum about wheelchairs, we might imagine a museum exploring the possibilities of movement. These kinds of initiatives "disturb" conventional perceptions through museum work of the highest quality.

As discussed in chapter 2, research shows that most visitors see exhibitions and museums as places that possess cultural authority, meaning that museums need to assume greater responsibility for their institutional choices. Perhaps contemporary art museums provide some of the most appropriate venues for reorienting public consciousness in this area, considering that many already have a reputation for questioning stereotypes and remain places where glamour, autonomy, and critical thinking converge.

The Accaparlante Cooperative offers another noteworthy example. This historical organization, based in Italy, aims at advocating for people with disabilities and has worked extensively at the MAMbo—*Museo d'Arte Moderna di Bologna* (Bologna's museum of contemporary art)—designing educational activities led by collaborators with cognitive disabilities. Their proposal is particularly successful in highlighting intersections between contemporary art and diversity, and it often uses irony and open dialogue as effective tools for challenging prejudices.[7]

It is crucial, in fact, that our projects strive to mitigate risks associated with images that can unwittingly jeopardize the potential impact of measures put into place. Despite the good intentions at the outset, these kinds of mistakes generate counterproductive effects in the long run. We need projects that make disability correctly visible on a symbolic and—most importantly—physical level as we steer clear of propagating damaging or inaccurate visions.

ENVISIONING THE FUTURE; BECOMING SPOKESPEOPLE

From this point of view, envisioning the future of accessibility is contingent on our ability to build a society in which this issue is regarded as a priority: Everyone needs it or will need it one day. Today's world is increasingly aware of its innate diversity. This discipline offers an important lens through which to redefine relationships and guarantee fair exchange and access to all.

For this reason, the hope is that museums act as trailblazers. With a clear understanding of the paradigms at play, museums already have the potential to act as models in a world where seeing should not be considered only as a visual ability, but any capacity to perceive. It is time for them to assume accountability for the quality of every visitor's experience and to bolster awareness about a multitude of needs. This process considers inclusivity front and center, whether redesigning a space for research and experimentation is a museum room, a set of captions, or a website.

We can all be spokespeople for people, the real center of all discourse pertaining to accessibility. Being a point person can take many forms: observing museums and their offerings; thinking about the needs of others; insisting on the diffusion of a critical knowledge set that emerges from direct, in-depth study and interaction with good practices; sharing the value of model cases; promoting evaluations; and sparking debate. Anyone whose work intersects with this discipline understands the indispensable role accessibility plays and recognizes the need to promote this field, ushering in a new and necessary future within the museum world and beyond.

THE TRAINING

The final training session consists of a workshop structured around a methodology called Open Space Technology. This is a familiar approach that works well as the closing session in a longer training course during which participants have had the opportunity to exchange ideas, rework complex content, and come up with concrete development prospects. For this reason, it is advisable to dedicate a full day to this activity (or no less than five hours), making sure you have the necessary space and skills to carry it out.

Workshop Objectives

1. Help participants re-elaborate what they have learned
2. Bring out and share critical issues
3. Generate motivation for action

Running the Workshop

Activity: Open Space Technology

Open Space Technology is a methodology designed for large groups, ranging from twenty to two thousand participants, and the activities involved can easily last an entire day, provided that the sessions are well planned. Developed by Harrison Owen, this method enables participants to freely share and discuss issues that matter most to them with their colleagues.[8] The four principles, outlined below, underpin the whole process and intend to motivate participants to guide themselves:

1. Whoever is present is the right person.
2. Whatever happens is the right turn of events.
3. Whenever it starts is the right time.
4. When it's over, it's over.

The activities begin with participants gathered in a circle. The facilitator, ideally an expert who is capable of remaining neutral, defines the time and space available, presents the topic for discussion, and shares the rules of the method. The choice of topic—and the statement used to sum it up—is key: It must be open and should inspire discussion without being too long or dry. In this case, this workshop should relate to themes dedicated to accessibility. Applying an approach "that invites interdisciplinary and inter-group thinking,"[9] an agenda is decided together with the participants who work in small groups to choose the issues for discussion.

At the end, the wall is covered with sessions and ideas, and the participants join the tables tackling the topics they find most interesting. If appropriate, the issues may also be reorganized in order of priority, and the groups can come together to discuss next steps, deadlines, and respective point people before the end of the event. At each table, the person who initially suggested the topic acts as facilitator, recording the points raised during the discussion on a flipchart. At the end of each session, participants can switch tables and explore another issue. It is important to incorporate breakout space and time, as well as providing plenty of flipcharts and pens. The facilitator should be present throughout to set the pace, to remind participants of the start and end of sessions, and to close the day's activities. At the end of the activity, you should allow at least thirty to forty minutes to read the compiled results on flipchart sheets, which should be displayed on one wall.

- Materials: flipcharts, markers, recording and reproduction equipment, and adhesive tape or magnets
- Preparation: for this activity, you will need a large room that easily accommodates all the groups, with wall space for displaying posters at the end

FINAL THOUGHTS

To make an impact, accessibility cannot merely be handed down from above. The whole museum must discuss and appropriate a shared vision stemming from intense dialogue and all-around commitment. Cultivating this awareness already helps to break down the widespread misconception that accessibility is difficult and unattainable. These simple measures will not, however, prove effective unless they form an integral part of a long-range process that engages a wealth of solutions geared to a broad spectrum of people who work in and visit museums. By adopting this approach, museums can guarantee their role as spaces that accommodate lifelong learning habits, cognizant of their audiences' morphing needs from childhood to old age. Their collections and care demonstrate to us that our only option is to embrace diversity.

NOTES

1. Heather Mariger, "Go Tell It on the Mountain: Spreading the Word about Your Accessibility Work," National Center on Disability and Access to Education, accessed July 6, 2021, https://ncdae.org/resources/articles/spreadingtheword.php.
2. Ibid.
3. "About Us," Museum, Arts and Culture Access Consortium, accessed July 6, 2021, https://macaccess.org/about-new/.
4. "About CCAC," Chicago Cultural Accessibility Consortium, accessed July 6, 2021, https://chicagoculturalaccess.org/about-us/.

5. "Chi siamo," Musei Toscani Alzheimer, accessed July 20, 2021, https://www.museitoscanialzheimer.org/chi-siamo.
6. Sara Hendren, "An Icon Is a Verb: About the Project," The Accessible Icon Project, February 2016, accessed February 24, 2021, https://accessibleicon.org/#an-icon-is-a-verb.
7. Lucia Cominioli, educator, *Cooperativa Accaparlante*, interview by author, Bologna, January 17, 2018.
8. Open Space Technology, accessed July 30, 2021, https://openspaceworld.org.
9. Ibid.

References

Abery, Nicola, Lenore Adler, and Anuradha Bhatia, eds. *The New Museum Community: Audiences, Challenges, Benefits*. Edinburgh: MuseumsEtc, 2010.

Abrams, Abigail. "30 Years after a Landmark Disability Law, the Fight for Access and Equality Continues." *Time*, July 23, 2020. https://time.com/5870468/americans-with-disabilities-act-coronavirus/.

Ackerson, Anne W., and Joan H. Baldwin. *Leadership Matters*. Nashville, TN: American Association for State and Local History, 2013.

Adams, Roxana. *Museums Visitor Service Manual*. Washington, DC: American Association of Museums, 2001.

American Alliance of Museums. "Definitions of Diversity, Equity, Accessibility, and Inclusion." Accessed April 2, 2021. https://www.aam-us.org/programs/diversity-equity-accessibility-and-inclusion/facing-change-definitions/.

American Alliance of Museums, "EdCom Newsletter." February 2016. https://www.aam-us.org/wp-content/uploads/2018/09/february-2016-newsletter.pdf.

American Alliance of Museums. *Evaluation in Diversity, Equity, Accessibility, and Inclusion Work: Lessons Learned from Museum Professionals Watch & Talk Host Guidelines*. July 2019. https://www.aam-us.org/wp-content/uploads/2019/07/Evaluation-in-DEAI-Work-host-guidelines-1.pdf.

American Alliance of Museums. *Facing Change: Insights from the American Alliance of Museums' Diversity, Equity, Accessibility, and Inclusions Working Group*. Arlington, VA: American Alliance of Museums, 2018.

American Alliance of Museums. "John Cotton Dana Award for Leadership." Accessed May 3, 2021. https://www.aam-us.org/programs/awards-competitions/john-cotton-dana-award-for-leadership.

American Association of Museums. *Mastering Civic Engagement: A Challenge to Museums*. Washington, DC: American Association of Museums, 2001.

American Association of Museums. *A Museums & Community Toolkit*. Washington, DC: American Association of Museums, 2002.

American Museum of Natural History. "Social Story for the American Museum of Natural History." Accessed July 18, 2021. https://www.amnh.org/content/download/323244/4997726/file/Social%20Story%20AMNH.pdf.

Anderson, Gail. *Reinventing the Museum: The Evolving Conversation on the Paradigm Shift*. 2nd ed. Lanham, MD: AltaMira Press, 2012.

Australian Museum. *Accessibility and Inclusion Action Plan 2018–2021: Providing Accessible and Inclusive Exhibits, Programs and Services*. Darlinghurst: Australian Museum, January 2018. https://media.australian.museum/media/dd/documents/australian-museum-accessibility-and-inclusion-action-plan-2018-2021-v2.77da658.pdf.

Bahram, Sina. "The Inclusive Museum." In *The Senses: Design Beyond Vision*, edited by Ellen Lupton and Andrea Lipps, 24–35. New York: Princeton Architectural Press, 2018.

Bahram, Sina, Susan Chun, and Anna Chiaretta Lavatelli. "Using Coyote to Describe the World." *MW18: Museums and the Web 2018*. April 17, 2018. https://mw18.mwconf.org/paper/using-coyote-to-describe-the-world/.

Benartzi, Shalom. *The Smarter Screen: Surprising Ways to Influence and Improve Online Behavior*. New York: Portfolio, 2015.

Bishop, Claire. *Radical Museology or, What's Contemporary in Museums of Contemporary Art?* London: Koening Books, 2014.

Bitgood, Stephen. "The Role of Attention in Designing Effective Interpretive Labels." *Journal of Interpretation Research* 5, no. 2 (November 1, 2000): 31–45. https://doi.org/10.1177/109258720000500205.

Bitgood, Stephen. *Social Design in Museums: The Psychology of Visitor Studies*. 2 vols. Edinburgh: MuseumEtc, 2011.

Black, Graham. *The Engaging Museum: Developing Museums for Visitor Involvement*. London: Routledge, 2005.

Black, Graham. *Museums and the Challenge of Change*. Abingdon, OX: Routledge, 2021. VitalSource Bookshelf.

Black, Graham. *Transforming Museums in the Twenty-First Century*. Abingdon, OX: Routledge, 2012.

Bollo, Alessandro. *Il museo e la conoscenza del pubblico: Gli studi sui visitatori*. Bologna: Istituto per i Beni artistici, culturali e naturali, 2004. https://online.ibc.regione.emilia-romagna.it/I/libri/pdf/bollo.pdf.

Bollo, Alessandro, and Luca dal Pozzolo. "Analysis of Visitor Behaviour inside the Museum: An Empirical Study." 2005. *Proceedings of the 8th International Conference on Arts and Cultural Management*, International Association of Arts and Cultural Management, Montreal, Canada, Article 28. http://neumann.hec.ca/aimac2005/PDF_Text/BolloA_DalPozzoloL.pdf.

Bourdieu, Pierre. *Distinction: A Social Critique of the Judgement of Taste*. Cambridge, MA: Harvard University Press, 1989.

Bourke, Juliet, and Andrea Titus. "Why Inclusive Leaders Are Good for Organizations, and How to Become One." *Harvard Business Review*, March 29, 2019. https://hbr.org/2019/03/why-inclusive-leaders-are-good-for-organizations-and-how-to-become-one.

Bradburne, James. *Interaction in the Museum: Observing, Supporting, Learning.* Self-published, Libri Books on Demand, 2000.

The British Museum. "Accessibility at the Museum." Accessed April 3, 2021. https://www.britishmuseum.org/visit/accessibility-museum.

Brook, Orian, Dave O'Brien, and Mark Taylor. *Culture Is Bad for You: Inequality in the Cultural and Creative Industries.* Manchester: Manchester University Press, 2020.

Byrne, John, Elinor Morgan, November Paynter, Aida Sánchez de Serdio, and Adela Železnik, eds. *The Constituent Museum. Constellations of Knowledge, Politics and Mediation: A Generator of Social Change.* Amsterdam: Valiz, 2018.

Cachia, Amanda. "Disability, Curating and the Educational Turn: The Contemporary Condition of Access in the Museum." *On-Curating*, Issue 24, 2014. https://www.on-curating.org/issue-24-reader/disability-curating-and-the-educational-turn-the-contemporary-condition-of-access-in-the-museum.html#.YTngw9OA4-R.

Calvard, Thomas. *Critical Perspectives on Diversity in Organizations.* New York: Routledge 2021.

Canadian Museum of Human Rights. "Accessibility." Accessed February 23, 2021. https://humanrights.ca/visit/accessibility.

Canadian Museum of Human Rights. "Inclusive and Accessible Guidelines." Accessed April 28, 2012. https://id.humanrights.ca/.

Canadian Museum of Human Rights. "Toward Greater Inclusion and Equity." Accessed June 21, 2021. https://humanrights.ca/about/toward-greater-inclusion-and-equity.

Carnegie Museums. "Overview | Accessibility Guidelines." Accessed April 15, 2021. http://web-accessibility.carnegiemuseums.org/.

Castello D'Albertis Museo delle Culture del Mondo. "Percorsi speciali." Accessed July 3, 2021. https://www.museidigenova.it/it/percorsi-speciali.

Catlin-Legutko, Cinnamon, and Stacy Klingler, eds. *Leadership, Mission, and Governance.* American Association for State and Local History Books. Walnut Creek, CA: AltaMira Press, 2013.

Catlin-Legutko, Cinnamon, and Stacy Klingler, eds. *Reaching and Responding to the Audience.* Walnut Creek, CA: AltaMira Press, 2013.

Chatterjee, Helen. *Touch in Museums: Policy and Practice in Object Handling.* Oxford: Berg, 2008.

Chicago Cultural Accessibility Consortium. "About CCAC." Accessed July 6, 2021. https://chicagoculturalaccess.org/about-us/.

Chick, Anne. "Co-creating an Accessible, Multisensory Exhibition with the National Centre for Craft & Design and Blind and Partially Sighted Participants." In *REDO: 2017 Cumulus International Conference*, 30 May–2 June 2017, Kolding Design School, Kolding Denmark. https://eprints.lincoln.ac.uk/id/eprint/27590/1/120_long_Chick-2%20%281%29.pdf.

Classen, Constance. *The Museum of the Senses: Experiencing Art and Collections.* London: Bloomsbury Academic, 2017.

Cock, Matthew. "Web Accessibility: Making Websites Accessible to All Is an Important Responsibility." *Museum Association Journal*, November 16, 2018. https://www.museumsassociation.org/museums-journal/in-practice/2018/11/16112018-web-accessibility-mp/.

Cole, Johnnetta B., and Laura L. Lott, eds. *Diversity, Equity, Accessibility and Inclusion in Museums.* American Alliance of Museums. Lanham, MD: Rowman & Littlefield, 2019.

Colombo, Maria Elena. *Musei e cultura digitale: Fra narrativa, pratiche e testimonianze.* Torino: Editrice Bibliografica, 2020.

Cooper Hewitt, Smithsonian Design Museum. "Access + Ability." Accessed April 11, 2021. https://www.cooperhewitt.org/channel/access-ability/.

Cooper Hewitt, Smithsonian Design Museum. "Cooper Hewitt Guidelines for Image Description." Accessed April 11, 2021. https://www.cooperhewitt.org/cooper-hewitt-guidelines-for-image-description/.

Cotton Dana, John. *The New Museum.* Woodstock, VT: ElmTree Press, 1917.

Coyote. "Case Study: MCA Chicago." Accessed April 12, 2021. https://coyote.pics/resources/case-study-mca-chicago/.

Crenshaw, Kimberlé. "Demarginalizing the Intersection of Race and Sex: A Black Feminist Critique of Antidiscrimination Doctrine, Feminist Theory and Antiracist Politics." University of Chicago Legal Forum 1 (8): 139–67, 1989.

Csikszentmihalyi, Mihaly. *Flow: The Psychology of Optimal Experience.* New York: Harper & Row, 1990.

Csikszentmihalyi, Mihaly, and Kim Hermanson. "Intrinsic Motivation in Museums: What Makes Visitors Want to Learn?" *Museum News* 74(3) (1995): 34–7, 59–62.

D'Alessio, Simona. "Disability Studies in Education: implicazioni per la ricerca educativa e la pratica scolastica italiana." In *Disability Studies, Emancipazione, inclusione scolastica e sociale, cittadinanza,* edited by Roberto Medeghini, Simona D'Alessio, Angelo Marra, Giuseppe Vadalà, and Enrico Valtellina, 89–124. Trento: Erickson, 2013.

Denscombe, Martyn. *Ground Rules for Social Research: Guidelines for Good Practice.* Maidenhead, Berkshire, UK: Open University Press, 2009.

Design Thinking for Museums. "Design Sprints for Content Development: How Phoenix Art Museum Ran a Design Sprint." Accessed April 2, 2021. https://designthinkingformuseums.net/2016/05/17/design-sprints-for-content-development.

Dewdney, Andrew, David Dibosa, and Victoria Walsh. *Post Critical Museology: Theory and Practice in the Art Museum.* London: Routledge, 2013.

Diamond, Judy, Jessica Luke, and David H. Uttal. *Practical Evaluation Guide: Tools for Museums and Other Informal Educational Settings.* Lanham, MD: AltaMira Press, 2009.

Dilenschneider, Colleen. "Active Visitors: Who Currently Attends Cultural Organizations?" *Colleen Dilenschneider: Know Your Own Bone.* January 23, 2019. https://www.colleendilen.com/2019/01/23/active-visitors-currently-attends-cultural-organizations-data/.

Disability Arts International. "The National Trust: Involving Disabled Users in Designing Access Features Can Be Transformative." Accessed February 23, 2021. https://www.disabilityartsinternational.org/resources/the-national-trust-involving-disabled-users-in-designing-access-features-can-be-transformative/.

Disability Visibility Project. Accessed May 1, 2021. https://disabilityvisibilityproject.com.

Dodd, Jocelyn, Richard Sandell, and Alison Coles. *Building Bridges: Guidance for Museums Galleries on Developing Audiences.* London: Museums and Galleries Commission, 1998.

Dodd, Jocelyn, Richard Sandell, Debbie Jolly, and Ceri Jones. *Rethinking Disability Representation in Museums and Galleries: Supporting Papers.* Leicester: Research Centre for Museums and Galleries (RCMG), University of Leicester, 2013. https://le.ac.uk/-/media/uol/docs/research-centres/rcmg/publications/rethinking-disability-representation-supporting-papers.pdf.

Downey, Stephanie. "Five Ways Evaluators Can Further Accessibility Efforts in Museums." *RK&A Learn with Us*, July 20, 2020. https://rka-learnwithus.com/five-ways-evaluators-can-further-accessibility-efforts-in-museums/.

Falk, John H. *Identity and the Museum Visitor Experience.* Walnut Creek, CA: Left Coast Press, Inc., 2009.

Falk, John H., and Lynn D. Dierking. *Learning from Museums: Visitor Experiences and the Making of Meaning.* Lanham, MD: AltaMira Press, 2020.

Falk, John H., and Lynn D. Dierking. *The Museum Experience.* London: Routledge, 2016.

Farrell, Betty, Maria Medvedeva, Cultural Policy Center NORC, and the Harris School of Public Policy at the University of Chicago. *Demographic Transformation and the Future of Museums.* Washington, DC: AAM Press American Association of Museums, 2010.

Finkel, Rebecca, Briony Sharp, and Majella Sweeney, eds. *Accessibility, Inclusion, and Diversity in Critical Event Studies.* London: Routledge, 2018.

Fleming, Neil D., and Coleen E. Mills. "Not Another Inventory, Rather a Catalyst for Reflection." *To Improve the Academy* 11, no. 1 (1992), 137–55. https://doi.org/10.1002/j.2334-4822.1992.tb00213.x.

Fondazione Medicina a Misura di Donna. Accessed July 21, 2021, https://www.medicinamisuradidonna.it/.

Foster, Harriet. *Evaluation Toolkit for Museum Practitioners.* Norwich: East of England Museum Hub, February 2008. https://visitors.org.uk/wp-content/uploads/2014/08/ShareSE_Evaltoolkit.pdf.

Gardner, Howard. *Frames of Mind: The Theory of Multiple Intelligences.* New York: Basic Books, 1983.

Garland-Thomson, Rosemarie. "Integrating Disability, Transforming Feminist Theory." *NWSA Journal* 14, no. 3 (2002), 1–32. https://www.jstor.org/stable/4316922?origin=JSTOR-pdf.

Garland-Thomson, Rosemarie. *Staring: How We Look.* Oxford: Oxford University Press, 2009.

Gilman, Benjamin Ives. "Museum Fatigue." *Scientific Monthly* 12 (1916), 62–74. https://www.jstor.org/stable/6127?seq=1#metadata_info_tab_contents.

Goodley, Dan. *Disability Studies: An Interdisciplinary Introduction*, 2nd ed. Thousand Oaks, CA: SAGE, 2017. Kindle.

Goodley, Dan. *Dis/ability Studies: Theorising Disablism and Ableism*. London: Routledge, 2014.

Google Arts & Culture. "Rijksmuseum." Accessed April 7, 2021. https://artsandculture.google.com/partner/rijksmuseum.

Graham, Helen. "Museums and How to Know about Access." *New Formations*, no. 79 (Autumn 2013), 64–81. https://www.academia.edu/7754903/Museums_and_How_to_Know_About_Access.

Grassini, Aldo, Andrea Socrati, and Annalisa Trasatti. *L'arte contemporanea e la scoperta dei valori della tattilità*. Roma: Armando Editore, 2018.

Gray, Dave, Sunni Brown, and James Macanufo. *Game Storming: A Playbook for Innovators, Rulebreakers, and Changemakers*. Sebastopol, CA: O'Reilly Media, 2010.

Güleç, Ayse, Claudia Hummel, Ulrich Schötker, and Wanda Wieczorek, eds. *Documenta 12 Education 1: Engaging Audiences, Opening Institutions: Methods and Strategies in Education at Documenta 12*. Berlin: Diaphanes, 2009.

Ham, Sam. *Interpretation: Making a Difference on Purpose*. Golden, CO: Fulcrum Publishing, 2016.

Hanes, Roy, Ivan Brown, and Nancy E. Hansen, eds. *The Routledge History of Disability*. London: Routledge, 2018.

Hayhoe, Simon. *Blind Visitor Experiences at Art Museums*. New York: Rowman & Littlefield, 2017.

Hayhoe, Simon. *Cultural Heritage, Aging, Disability, and Identity*. London: Routledge, 2019.

Heath, Christian, and Maurice Davies. "Why Evaluation Doesn't Measure Up." *Museum Journal*. June 2012. https://www.museumsassociation.org/museums-journal/opinion/2012/06/01062012-why-evaluation-doesnt-measure-up/#.

Hein, George E. *Learning in the Museum*. Abingdon, OX: Routledge, 1998.

Hein, George E. "Is Meaning Making Constructivism? Is Constructivism Meaning Making?" *Exhibitionist* 18, no. 2 (1999), 15–18. http://www.george-hein.com/downloads/Hein_isMeaningMaking.pdf.

Hendren, Sara. "An Icon Is a Verb: About the Project." The Accessible Icon Project. February 2016. https://accessibleicon.org/#an-icon-is-a-verb.

Hennes, Tom. "Rethinking the Visitor Experience." *Curator: The Museum Journal* 45, no. 2 (2002), 105–17. https://doi.org/10.1111/cura.2002.45.issue-1.

Hill Collins, Patricia, and Sirma Bilge. *Intersectionality*. Cambridge: Polity Press, 2016.

Hogart, Brian. "Rethinking Curator/Educator Training and Interaction in the Co-Production of Art Museum Exhibitions." In *Visitor-Centered Exhibitions and Edu-Curation in Art Museums*, edited by Pat Villeneuve and Ann Rowson Love, 23–44. Lanham, MD: Rowman & Littlefield, 2017. Kindle.

Holmes, Kat. *Mismatch: How Inclusion Shapes Design.* Cambridge: The MIT Press, 2020.

Hooper-Greenhill, Eilean, ed. *The Educational Role of the Museum.* London: Routledge, 1994.

Hooper-Greenhill, Eilean. *Museum, Media, Message.* London: Routledge, 1999.

Hooper-Greenhill, Eilean. "Studying Visitors." In *A Companion to Museum Studies*, edited by Susan McDonald, 362–76. Malden, MA: Blackwell Publishing, Ltd., 2006.

Horton, Sarah. "Digital Accessibility and Disability Inclusion." *Sarah Horton Design* (blog), August 10, 2014. https://sarahhortondesign.com/2014/08/10/organizations-accessibility-and-change.

Hughes, Philippe. *Exhibition Design.* London: Laurence King Publishing, 2010.

Huybrechts, Liesbeth, ed. *Participation Is Risky: Approaches to Joint Creative Processes.* Amsterdam: Valiz, 2013.

Iyer, Jenee. "New Apps Focus on Autism Inclusivity." *Arts Management and Technology Laboratory.* March 17, 2017. https://amt-lab.org/reviews/2017/2/new-apps-focus-on-autism-inclusivity.

Janes, Robert R. *Museums and the Paradox of Change.* 3rd ed. London: Routledge, 2013.

Janes, Robert R., and Richard Sandell, eds. *Museum Activism.* London: Routledge, 2019.

Jung, Yuha. "Toward a Learning Museum and System Intelligence." In *System Thinking in Museums: Theory and Practice*, edited by Yuha Jung and Ann Rowson Love, 219–28. Lanham, MD: Rowman & Littlefield, 2017.

Jung, Yuha, and Ann Rowson Love, eds. *Systems Thinking in Museums: Theory and Practice.* Lanham, MD: Rowman & Littlefield, 2017.

Kahneman, Daniel. *Thinking, Fast and Slow.* London: Penguin Ramdom House, 2012.

The Kids Are All Right. Accessed May 1, 2021. http://www.thekidsareallright.org/.

Kinard, John. "The Museum in the Service of Man Today and Tomorrow." Paper from the Ninth General Conference of ICOM, 151–156, Paris, ICOM, 1972.

Klinenberg, Eric. *Palaces for the People: How Social Infrastructure Can Help Fight Inequality, Polarization, and the Decline of Civic Life.* New York City: Broadway Books, 2019.

Kudlick, Catherine, and Edward M. Luby. "Access as Activism: Bringing the Museum to the People." In *Museum Activism*, edited by Robert R. Janes and Richard Sandell, 58–68. London: Routledge, 2019.

Lang, Caroline, John Reeve, and Vicky Woollard, eds. *The Responsive Museum: Working with Audiences in the Twenty-First Century.* London: Routledge, 2017.

Levent, Nina, and Alvaro Pascual-Leone, eds. *The Multisensory Museum: Cross-Disciplinary Perspectives on Touch, Sounds, Smell, Memory, and Space.* Lanham, MD: Rowman & Littlefield, 2014. Kindle.

Lewrick, Micheal, Patrick Link, and Larry Leifer. *The Design Thinking Toolbox: A Guide to Mastering the Most Popular and Valuable Innovative Methods.* Hoboken, NJ: Wiley, 2020.

Lidwell, William, Kritina Holden, and Jill Butler. *Universal Principles of Design: 125 Ways to Enhance Usability, Influence Perception, Increase Appeal, Make Better Design Decisions, and Teach through Design.* 2nd ed. Beverly, MA: Rockport Publishers, 2010.

Linzer, Danielle, Desi Gonzalez, and Sina Bahram. "Warhol for All: Designing an Inclusive Audio Guide and Tactile Exhibition Elements at The Andy Warhol Museum." In *Inclusive Digital Interactives: Best Practices + Research*, edited by Beth Ziebarth, Janice Majewski, Robin Marquis, and Nancy Proctor, 243–64. Washington, DC: Access Smithsonian, Institute for Human Centered Design and MuseWeb, 2020. https://access.si.edu/sites/default/files/inclusive-digital -interactives-best-practices-research.pdf.

Louise, Dany. *The Interpretation Matters Handbook.* London: Black Dog Press, 2015.

Lupton, Ellen. *Beautiful Users: Designing for People.* Hudson, NY: Princeton Architectural Press, 2014.

Lupton, Ellen, and Andrea Lipps, eds. *The Senses: Design beyond Vision.* Hudson, NY: Princeton Architectural Press, 2018.

Lynch, Bernadette. "I'm Gonna Do Something: Moving beyond Talk in the Museum." In *Museum Activism*, edited by Robert R. Janes and Richard Sandell, 115–26. London: Routledge, 2019.

Lynch, Bernadette. *Whose Cake Is It Anyway? A Collaborative Investigation into Engagement and Participation in Twelve Museums and Galleries in the UK.* London: Paul Hamlyn Foundation, 2011. https://www.phf.org.uk/publications/whose-cake-anyway.

Majewski, Janice, and Lonnie Bunch. "The Expanding Definition of Diversity: Accessibility and Disability Culture Issues in Museum Exhibitions." *Curator* 41, no. 3 (1998), 153–61. https://doi.org/10.1111/j.2151-6952.1998.tb00829.x.

Malandain Beth, Christine Reich, Jessica Ghelichi, Leigh Ann Mesiti Caulfield, and Julia Tate. "An Ongoing Experiment: Developing Inclusive Digital Interactives at a Science Museum." In *Inclusive Digital Interactives: Best Practices + Research*, edited by Beth Ziebarth, Janice Majewski, Robin Marquis, and Nancy Proctor, 243–64. Washington, DC: Access Smithsonian, Institute for Human Centered Design and MuseWeb, 2020. https://access.si.edu/sites/default/files/inclusive-digital -interactives-best-practices-research.pdf.

Mariger, Heather. "Go Tell It on the Mountain: Spreading the Word about Your Accessibility Work." The National Center on Disability and Access to Education. Accessed July 6, 2021. https://ncdae.org/resources/articles/spreadingtheword .php.

Marrall, Rebecca M. *Developing a Library Accessibility Plan: A Practical Guide for Librarians.* London: Rowman & Littlefield, 2020.

Marshall, Alex. "Is This the World's Most Accessible Museum?" *New York Times*, updated September 11, 2019. http://www.nytimes.com/2019/09/06/arts/de sign/disabled-access-wellcome-collection.html.

Marstine, Janet, ed. *The Routledge Companion to Museum Ethics. Redefining Ethics for the Twenty-First-Century Museum.* London: Routledge, 2011.

McKenna-Cress, Polly, and Janet Kamien. *Creating Exhibitions: Collaboration in the Planning, Development, and Design of Innovative Experiences.* Hoboken, NJ: Wiley, 2013.

Merritt, Elizabeth. "Trust Me, I'm a Museum." *Centre for the Future of Museums Blog,* February 3, 2015. https://www.aam-us.org/2015/02/03/trust-me-im-a -museum/.

The Metropolitan Museum of Art. "Accessibility." Accessed February 23, 2021. www.metmuseum.org/visit/accessibility.

The Metropolitan Museum of Art. "Bulletin of the Metropolitan Museum of Art" 8, no. 5 (1913).

The Metropolitan Museum of Art. "My Met Tour." Accessed May 16, 2021. https:// www.metmuseum.org/-/media/files/events/programs/progs-for-visitors -with-disabilities/my-met-tour.pdf.

The Metropolitan Museum of Art. "Plan Your Visit." Accessed April 7, 2021. https:// www.metmuseum.org/visit/plan-your-visit.

The Metropolitan Museum of Art. "Annual Report for the Year 2018–2019." November 12, 2019. https://www.metmuseum.org/-/media/files/about-the -met/annual-reports/2018-2019/annual-report-2018-19.pdf?la=en&hash= CA4A390302ED38ACB2EB9ACEBB7B80E6.

Meuser, Philipp, Daniela Pogade, and Jennifer Tobolla, eds. *Accessibility and Wayfinding Manual. Construction and Design Manual.* Berlin: DOM Publisher, 2019.

Microsoft. "Microsoft Inclusive Design Booklet." Accessed April 11, 2021. https:// www.microsoft.com/design/inclusive/.

Mohn, Tanya. "Welcoming Art Lovers with Disabilities." *New York Times,* October 25, 2013. https://www.nytimes.com/2013/10/27/arts/artsspecial/welcom ing-art-lovers-with-disabilities.html.

Moore, Porchia. "The Danger of the 'D' Word: Museums and Diversity." *Incluseum* (blog), January 2014. https://incluseum.com/2014/01/20/the-danger-of-the -d-word-museums-and-diversity/.

Mörsch, Carmen, eds. *Documenta 12 Education 2: Between Critical Practice and Visitor Services Results of a Research Project.* Berlin: Diaphanes, 2009.

Murawski, Mike. *Museums and Agents of Change: A Guide to Becoming a Changemaker.* Lanham, MD: Rowman & Littlefield, 2020.

MUSAC. *Working from Diversity: Learning Experiences through Art of the Present.* Barcelona: Actar, 2010.

Musei Toscani per l'Alzheimer. "Chi siamo." Accessed July 20, 2021. https://www .museitoscanialzheimer.org/chi-siamo/.

Museum, Arts and Culture Access Consortium (MAC). "About Us." Accessed June 21, 2021. https://macaccess.org/about-new/.

Museum, Arts and Culture Access Consortium (MAC). "Meet Our Grants: Mapping Virtual Access in Cultural Institutions." Accessed June 21, 2021. https://macaccess .org/meet-our-grants-mapping-virtual-access-in-cultural-institutions/.

Museum of Contemporary Art Australia. "Celebrating Difference: Access, Diversity and Inclusion Plan 2018–2020." Accessed June 22, 2021. https://www.mca.com.au/about-us/reports-and-policies/access-diversity-and-inclusion-plan-20182020/.

Museum of London. "Museum Accessibility." Accessed May 23, 2021. https://www.museumoflondon.org.uk/museum-london/plan-your-visit/museum-accessibility.

Museum of Modern Art. "Museum Training Resources | MoMA." Accessed April 7. 2021, https://www.moma.org/visit/accessibility/resources.

Museum of Modern Art. "Meet Me at MoMA. The MoMA Alzheimer's Project." Accessed June 9, 2021. https://www.moma.org/visit/accessibility/meetme/.

MuseumsEtc. *10 must Reads: Inclusion. Empowering New Audiences.* Edinburgh: MuseumsEtc, 2014.

The Museums, Libraries and Archives Council. "Access for All Self-Assessment Toolkit: Checklist 1, Disability Access for Museums, Libraries and Archives." January 8, 2006. www.ne-mo.org/fileadmin/Dateien/public/topics/Disability_and_museums/disability_checklist_pdf_6540.pdf.

Museum of Science of Boston and Art Beyond Sight. "Guide to Conducting Formative Evaluation on Accessible Programming." November 2013. www.artbeyondsight.org/mei/formative-evaluation-of-accessible-programming/.

Nati con la Cultura. Accessed July 21, 2021. http://www.naticonlacultura.it.

National Endowment for the Arts. "Accessibility Planning and Resource Guide for Cultural Administrators." 2011. https://www.arts.gov/impact/accessibility/publications-checklists-and-resources/accessibility-planning-and-resource-guide-cultural-administrators.

National Endowment for the Arts. "Design for Accessibility: A Cultural Administrators Handbook." 2003. https://www.arts.gov/sites/default/files/Design-for-Accessibility.pdf.

Network of European Museum Organisations (NEMO). "Survey on the Impact of the COVID-19 Situation on Museums in Europe, Final Report." December 5, 2020. https://www.nemo.org/fileadmin/Dateien/public/NEMO_documents/NEMO_COVID19_Report_12.05.2020.pdf.

Newman, Dan. *From the Front of the Room: Notes on Facilitation for Experienced Practitioners.* Roma: Matter Group, 2015.

The New School. "A Museum for Everyone." Accessed June 20, 2021. https://www.newschool.edu/pressroom/pressreleases/2013/ParsonsandTheMetropolitanMuseumofArt.htm.

Nielsen, Tina C., and Lisa Kepinski. *Inclusion Nudges for Motivating Allies in All Organizations and Communities.* Self-published, 2020.

Of/By/For All. "Who's Coming? Respectful Audience Surveying Toolkit." 2019. https://static1.squarespace.com/static/5a8e0a68f9a61e43fb3eb0e2/t/5d0cf607a5ad8200016a8b06/1561130515568/OFBYFOR_ALL_Respectful_Audience_Surveying_Toolkit.pdf._

Open Space Technology. Accessed July 30, 2021. https://openspaceworld.org.

Oregon Arts Commission. "Accessibility for Under 100 Dollars." Accessed February 23, 2021. https://www.oregonartscommission.org/publications-and-resources/accessibility-under-100-dollars.

Parry, Ross, Ruth Page, and Alex Moseley, eds. *Museum Thresholds: The Design and Media of Arrival.* London: Routledge, 2020.

Pater, Ruben. *The Politics of Design: A (Not So) Global Manual for Visual Communication.* Amsterdam: BIS Publishers, 2016.

Paul Hamlyn Foundation. "Our Museum: Communities and Museums as Active Partners." Accessed April 29, 2021. http://ourmuseum.org.uk/.

Perry, Deborah. *What Makes Learning Fun? Principles for the Design of Intrinsically Motivating Museum Exhibits.* Lanham, MD: Rowman Altamira, 2012.

Pitman, Bonnie, and Ellen Cochran Hirzy. *Ignite the Power of Art: Advancing Visitor Engagement in Museums.* New Haven, CT: Yale University Press, 2011.

Pressman, Heather, and Danielle Schulz. *The Art of Access: A Practical Guide for Museum Accessibility.* Lanham, MD: Rowman & Littlefield, 2021.

Pulling, Graham. *Design Meets Disability.* Cambridge, MA: MIT Press, 2009.

Rand, Judy. "Visitors' Bill of Rights." In *Museums Visitor Service Manual*, edited by Roxana Adams, 13–14. Washington, DC: American Association of Museums, 2001.

Ravelli, Louise J. *Museum Texts: Communication Frameworks.* London: Routledge, 2006.

Rayner, Ann. *Access in Mind: Towards the Inclusive Museum.* Edinburgh: Intellectual Access Trust, 1998.

Reilly, Maura. *Curatorial Activism: Towards an Ethics of Curating.* London: Thames & Hudson, 2018.

Remotti, Francesco. *Somiglianze: Una via per la convivenza.* Bari: Laterza, 2020.

Richardson, Jim. "Can Flatter Organisational Structures Work for Museums?" *Museum Next,* October 23, 2019. http://www.museumnext.com/article/can-flatter-organisational-structures-work-for-museums/.

Roberts, Louise. *From Knowledge to Narrative: Educators and the Changing Museum.* Washington, DC: Smithsonian Institution Press, 1997.

Rodney, Seph. *The Personalization of the Museum Visit: Art Museums, Discourse, and Visitors.* London: Routledge, 2018. Kindle.

Romano, Alessandra. *Diversity and Disability Management: Esperienze di inclusione sociale.* Milano: Mondadori, 2020.

Roppola, Tiina. *Designing for the Museum Visitor Experience.* New York: Routledge, 2011. Kindle.

Salmen, John P. S. *Everyone's Welcome: The Americans with Disabilities Act and Museums.* Washington, DC: American Association of Museums, 1998. https://files.eric.ed.gov/fulltext/ED437754.pdf.

Sandell, Richard. *Museums, Prejudice and the Reframing of Difference.* Abingdon, OX: Routledge, 2006.

Sandell, Richard, and Annie Delin. "In the Shadow of the Freakshow: The Impact of Freakshow Tradition on the Display and Understanding of Disability History in Museums." *Disability Studies Quarterly*, 4, no. 25 (Fall 2005). https://dsq-sds.org/article/view/614/791.

Sandell, Richard, Jocelyn Dodd, and Rosemarie Garland-Thomson, eds. *Re-Presenting Disability: Activism and Agency in the Museum*. London: Routledge, 2013.

Sandell, Richard, and Eithne Nightingale, eds. *Museums, Equality and Social Justice*. London: Routledge, 2012.

Schianchi, Matteo. *La terza nazione del mondo: i disabili tra pregiudizio e realtà*. Milano: Feltrinelli, 2009.

Schilp, Erik, and Jasper Visser. *Quantum Culture*. Amsterdam: VSSCH + STAM, 2018.

Schonfeld, Roger, and Liam Sweeney. "Organizing the Work of the Art Museum." *Ithaka S+R*. Last modified July 10, 2019. https://doi.org/10.18665/sr.311731.

Schrøder, Kim Christian, Kirsten Drotner, Stephen Kline, and Catherine Murray. *Researching Audiences: A Practical Guide to Methods in Media Audience Analysis*. London: Bloomsbury Academic, 2003.

Sclavi, Marianella, and Lawrence E. Susskind. *Confronto creative: Dal diritto di parola al diritto di essere ascoltati*. Milano et al., 2011.

Serrell, Beverly. *Exhibit Labels: An Interpretive Approach*. 2nd ed. Lanham, MD: Rowman & Littlefield, 2015.

Shakespeare, Tom. *Disabilità e società: Diritti, falsi miti, percezioni sociali*. Trento: Erikson, 2017.

Shakespeare, Tom. *Disability: The Basics*. London: Routledge, 2017.

Shepley, Emma. "Advancing Disability Equality through Cultural Institutions." Research Centre for Museums and Galleries (RCMG), *Research Impact Report*. Spring 2020. https://le.ac.uk/rcmg/reframing-difference-and-disability.

Siebers, Tobin. *Disability Aesthetics*. Ann Arbor, MI: Michigan Press, 2010.

Silverman, Lois H. "Making Meaning Together: Lessons from the Field of American History." In *Transforming Practice: Selections from the Journal of Museum Education, 1992-1999*, edited by Joanne S. Hirsch and Lois H. Silverman. London: Routledge, 2006.

Silverman, Lois H. "Meaning Making Matters: Communication, Consequences, and Exhibit Design." *Exhibitionist* 18, no. 2 (1999), 8–14.

Silverman, Lois H. *The Social Work of Museums*. London: Routledge, 2010.

Simon, Nina. *The Art of Relevance*. Santa Cruz, CA: Museum 2.0, 2016.

Simon, Nina. *The Participatory Museum*. Santa Cruz, CA: Museum 2.0, 2010.

Sinek, Simon. *Start with Why: How Great Leaders Inspire Everyone to Take Action*. New York: Penguin Press, 2009.

Slack, Steven. *Interpreting Heritage: A Guide to Planning and Practice*. London: Routledge, 2021.

Smed, Sarah. "Behind Barbed Wire: Co-producing the Danish Welfare Museum." In *Museums and Social Change: Challenging the Unhelpful Museum*, edited by Adele

Chynoweth, Bernadette Lynch, Klaus Petersen, and Sarah Smed, 35–47. London: Routledge, 2020. VitalSource Bookshelf.

Smith, Heather J. L., Barry Gingley, and Hanna Goodwin. "Beyond Compliance? Museums, Disability and the Law." In *Museums, Equality and Social Justice*, edited by Richard Sandell and Eithne Nightingale, 59–71. London: Routledge, 2012.

Smithsonian Accessibility Program. "Smithsonian Guidelines for Accessible Exhibition Design." Revised March 2011. https://www.sifacilities.si.edu/sites/default/files/Files/Accessibility/accessible-exhibition-design1.pdf.

Sousa, Hugo, and Maria Vlachou. *The Cultural Participation of People with Disabilities or Impairments: How to Create an Accessibility Plan.* Lisbon: Cámara Municipal, 2020. https://accesscultureportugal.files.wordpress.com/2021/03/manual_access_plan.pdf.

Starr, Ruth. "Prioritizing Image Descriptions and Digital Equity at Cooper Hewitt." *American Alliance on Museums*, May 13, 2020. https://www.aam-us.org/2020/05/13/prioritizing-image-descriptions-and-digital-equity-at-cooper-hewitt/.

Steinfeld, Edward, and Jordana Maisel. *Universal Design: Creating Inclusive Environments.* Hoboken, NJ: Wiley, 2012.

Stickdorn, Marc, and Jakob Schneider. *This Is Service Design Thinking: Basics, Tools, Cases.* Hoboken, NJ: Wiley, 2012.

Stringer, Katie. "Disability, the Sideshow, and Modern Museum Practices." *Scientia et Humanitas* 3 (2013), 15–28. https://libjournals.mtsu.edu/index.php/scientia/article/view/551.

Stringer, Katie. "The Legacy of Dime Museums and the Freakshow: How the Past Impacts the Present." *American Association for State and Local History*, Autumn 2013. https://aaslh.org/the-legacy-of-dime-museums-and-the-freakshow-how-the-past-impacts-the-present/.

Stringer, Katie. *Programming for People with Special Needs: A Guide for Museums and Historic Sites.* Lanham, MD: Rowman & Littlefield/AASLH, 2014.

Tavin, Kevin, and Hiltunen Mirja, eds. *Experimenting Fads: Finnish Art-Education Doctoral Studies.* Espoo, Finland: Aalto University, 2017.

Thaler, Richard H., and Cass R. Sunstein. *Nudge: Improving Decisions about Health, Wealth and Happiness.* London: Penguin Books Ltd., 2008.

Thomas, David A., and Robin J. Ely. "Making Difference Matter: A New Paradigm for Managing Diversity." In *On Diversity*, edited by *Harvard Business Review*, 1–28. Boston: Harvard Business Review Press, 2019.

Tilden, Freeman. *Interpreting Our Heritage.* 3rd ed. Chapel Hill, NC: University of North Carolina Press, 1977.

Tilden, Freeman. *Practices for Visitor Services in Parks, Museums, and Historic Places.* Chapel Hill, NC: North Carolina Press, 2008.

Trofanenko, Brenda, and Avner Segall, eds. *Beyond Pedagogy: Reconsidering the Public Purpose of Museums.* Rotterdam: Sense Publisher, 2014.

TV 2 PLAY. "TV 2 | All That We Share." YouTube Video, 3:00. January 27, 2017. https://www.youtube.com/watch?v=jD8tjhVO1Tc.

U.S. Department of Justice, Civil Rights Division. "ADA | Maintaining Accessibility in Museums." Accessed April 21, 2021. https://www.ada.gov/business/museum_access.htm.

Van Heusden, Barend, and Pascal Gielen, eds. *Arts Education beyond Art: Teaching Art in Times of Change.* Amsterdam: Valiz, 2015.

Van Mensch, Peter, and Léontine Meijer-Van Mensch. *New Trends in Museology.* Celje, Slovenia: Celje Museum of Recent History, 2011.

Vermeeren, Arnold, Licia Calvi, and Amalia Sabiescu, eds. *Museum Experience Design Crowds, Ecosystems and Novel Technologies.* New York City: Springer, 2018.

Verwayen, Harry, Julia Fallon, Julia Schellenberg, and Panagiotis Kyrou, eds. *Impact Playbook for Museums, Libraries, Archives, and Galleries.* Den Haag: Europeana Foundation. 2017.

Veverka, John A. *The Interpretive Trails Book: Effective Planning and Design.* Edinburgh: MuseumsEtc, 2015.

Veverka, John A. *Interpretive Training Handbook: Content, Strategies, Tips, Handouts and Practical Learning Experiences for Teaching Interpretation to Others.* Edinburgh: MuseumsEtc, 2011.

Villeneuve, Pat, and Ann Rowson Love. *Visitor-Centered Exhibitions and Edu-Curation in Art Museums.* Lanham, MD: Rowman & Littlefield, 2017. Kindle.

Visocky O'Grady, Jenn, and Ken Visocky O'Grady. *A Designer's Research Manual.* 2nd ed. Beverly, MA: Rockport, 2017.

Watson, Nick, and Simo Vehmas. *Routledge Handbook of Disability Studies.* 2nd. ed. Abingdon, OX: Routledge, 2020.

Watson, Sheila, ed. *Museums and Their Communities.* London: Routledge, 2007.

Weil, Stephen E. *Making Museums Matter.* Washington, DC: Smithsonian Books, 2002.

Weil, Stephen E. "From Being about Something to Being for Somebody: The Ongoing Transformation of the American Museum." *Daedalus* 128, no. 3 (1999), 229–58. https://www.jstor.org/stable/20027573.

Weinschenk, Susan. *100 Things Every Designer Needs to Know about People.* San Francisco: New Riders, 2011.

Weisen, Marcus. "From the Margins to the Core?" in *Sackler Conference for Arts Education* (Wednesday, March 24–Friday, March 26, 2010). http://media.vam.ac.uk/media/documents/conferences/2010/margins-to-the-core/v&a-fromthemarginstothecore-compiledpapers&notes.pdf.

Weisen, Marcus. *International Perspectives on the Cultural Accessibility of People with Disabilities: A Project Access White Paper.* New York: Art Beyond Sight, 2012. http://www.artbeyondsight.org/mei/wp-content/uploads/WP_International _Perspectives-REV.pdf.

Wheeler, Jo, and Amber Walls. *Envision: A Handbook: Supporting Young People's Participation in Galleries and the Arts.* London: Engage, 2008.

Whitehead, Christopher. *Interpreting Art in Museums and Galleries.* London: Routledge, 2011.

World Health Organization. "Disability and Health." Accessed March 21, 2021. https://www.who.int/news-room/fact-sheets/detail/disability-and-health.

World Wide Web Consortium. "Web Accessibility Initiative (WAI)." Accessed April 8, 2021. https://www.w3.org/WAI/.

Wyman Bruce, Corey Timpson, Scott Gillam, and Sina Bahram. "Inclusive Design: From Approach to Execution." *MW2016: Museums and the Web 2016*, February 24, 2016. https://mw2016.museumsandtheweb.com/paper/inclusive-design -from-approach-to-execution.

Ziebarth, Beth, Janice Majewski, Robin Marquis, and Nancy Proctor, eds. *Inclusive Digital Interactives: Best Practices + Research*. Washington, DC: Access Smithsonian, Institute for Human Centered Design and MuseWeb, 2020. https://access .si.edu/sites/default/files/inclusive-digital-interactives-best-practices-research .pdf.

Index

About the Author

Maria Chiara Ciaccheri is a museum consultant, researcher, and docent. With a background in museum studies and management and an MA in learning and visitor studies in museums from the University of Leicester (UK), over the last fifteen years she has worked and researched extensively in the field of museum accessibility, with focus on cognitive issues, disability representation, and participatory approaches in adult education.

As a recipient of private and public grants since 2014, she has traveled and researched across the United States, mapping and observing more than a hundred accessible best practices throughout the country. Her field research has continued over the following years, as she visited and investigated as many museums and best practices in accessibility as possible, both in Italy and in greater Europe. As a lecturer in museum accessibility for a number of post-graduate university programs in Italy and the author of various articles and publications, she often speaks at national and international conferences.

She works as a consultant with several organizations and museums and is particularly interested in strategic and organizational processes. Most recently, she launched the Museums for People project (museumsforpeople.com) to support museum studies and the dissemination and awareness of accessibility through illustrations and simplified language. Her personal website is mariachiaraciaccheri. com.